# Bible Detectives
# Exodus

## FUN BIBLE STUDIES USING PUZZLES & STORIES

## Written by Ros Woodman
## Illustrated by Ron Wheeler

**Cover Design by J Sherlock**        **Illustration Ron Wheeler**
**Printed and bound by Bell and Bain**
**Published by Christian Focus Publications**
**Geanies House, Fearn, Tain, Ross-shire, IV20 1TW, Scotland, UK.**
**www.christianfocus.com  email: info@christianfocus.com ISBN: 1-84550-067-9**

## INTRODUCTION

Hello. We're Harry and Jess. We're the Bible Detectives and we're on a special case. We're on an investigation through the second book of the Bible – Exodus – and we've got Click, our computer mouse to help. Before we start, Click has downloaded data to get us started.

## The Bible

This is God's book. He used people to do physical writing. Prophets, men of God, the disciples – all wrote down or told other people what God said to them. There are two sections. The Old Testament happened before Jesus was born and the New Testament is about Jesus life, death, resurrection and what his followers did after he went back to heaven.

## More Data

The Old and New Testaments are divided into different sections. The Old Testament is the first section of the Bible and is made up of 39 separate books. The New Testament is made up of 27 books. Each book is divided into smaller sections called chapters. Each chapter is divided into smaller parts called verses.

## Exodus

The book of Genesis finishes with Jacob's family moving to the land of Egypt. But the opening scene of Exodus takes place 350 years later and things have changed for Jacob's family - and not for the better. Now we find that hundreds of thousands of Jacob's ancestors are working as slaves for the Egyptian task masters. They are working on huge construction projects. It is back breaking work. The book of Exodus then is the story of these people and their God and how he delivers them from slavery. But that is only part of the story. There is a long journey and many dangers along the way for the Hebrew people to face but most importantly they have a lot to learn about the God who has chosen them and who is leading them to a new land. They had lots to learn - and so do we!

## Old Testament

Genesis, Exodus, Leviticus, Numbers, Deuteronomy, Joshua, Judges, Ruth, 1 & 2 Samuel, 1 & 2 Kings, 1 & 2 Chronicles, Ezra, Nehemiah, Esther, Job, Psalms, Proverbs, Ecclesiastes, Song of Songs, Isaiah, Jeremiah, Lamentations, Ezekiel, Daniel, Hosea, Joel, Amos, Obadiah, Jonah, Micah, Nahum, Habakkuk, Zephaniah, Haggai, Zechariah, Malachi.

## New Testament:

Matthew, Mark, Luke, John, Acts, Romans, 1 & 2 Corinthians, Galatians, Ephesians, Philippians, Colossians, 1 & 2 Thessalonians, 1 & 2 Timothy, Titus, Philemon, Hebrews, James, 1 & 2 Peter, 1, 2 & 3 John, Jude, Revelation.

That's great, Click. Thanks for showing us that. So, come on everyone – pick up a pencil, and let's go.

# Study One: The Israelites in Egypt

It's fun being a Bible detective. There are so many new things to discover about God and his plan for people throughout history. Are you ready to check out the book of Exodus with us? Then, let's go!

Click has been helping us to recall what happened at the very end of the book of Genesis. We learned about a Hebrew called Joseph, who lived in the land of Canaan. He had eleven brothers and they hated him because he was their father Jacob's favourite son. So, who were the brothers? Click has printed out a key to help us work it out.

a =1, b = 2, c = 3 etc

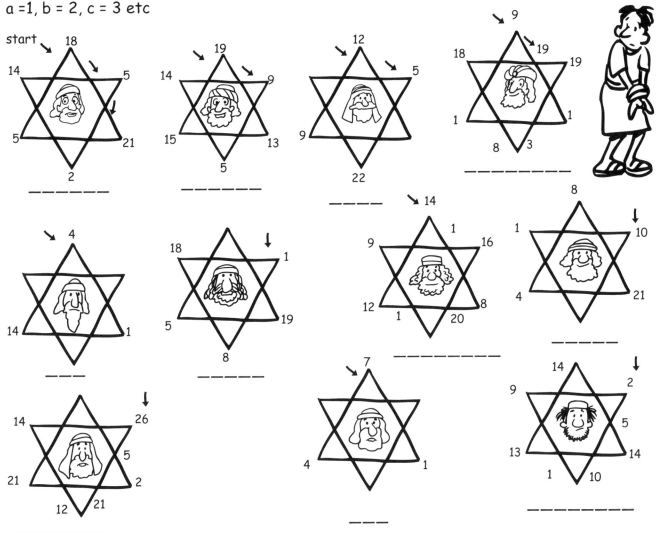

Joseph's brothers sold him into slavery in Egypt, but after a while, God brought him to Pharaoh's notice. Pharaoh was the king of that land and he had had a dream which had really troubled him. Only Joseph could tell him the meaning of it – that there were going to be seven years of bumper harvests, followed by seven years of famine. Pharaoh was so impressed with Joseph that he made him the next most important person in Egypt after himself. We discovered that God had been in control all along, and in the end, he made it possible for Joseph to be reunited with his brothers and his father.

Joseph forgave his brothers. He knew that God had allowed everything to happen so that his family could be saved from starvation when the famine came. Joseph moved his whole family to the land of Egypt – and now the book of Exodus begins. Click's printed us out a puzzle on the next page. Can you fill in the gaps to update us on the situation in Egypt?

Joseph and his brothers 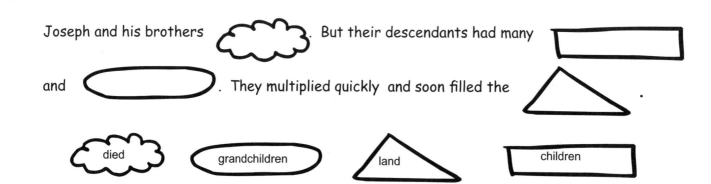 But their descendants had many and _____. They multiplied quickly and soon filled the _____.

died    grandchildren    land    children

A new king came to the throne of Egypt. He didn't know anything about Joseph or what he had done. He simply took note of all the Israelites living in the land and felt threatened.

So the Egyptians made the Israelites their slaves and treated them very harshly. They forced them to build two cities as supply centres for the king. Let's investigate. Take the first letter of each picture to find out what the cities were called.

If we don't put an end to this, if war breaks out, they will join our enemies and fight against us.

1

and

2

It's a strange thing, but our research shows that the worse the Egyptians treated the Israelites, the more they grew in number. This was far too threatening, and further action had to be taken. Click has discovered some pictures to show us what the Egyptians did.

The Egyptians were so alarmed, they decided to make life even more unbearable for the slaves.

They were ruthless, forcing the Israelites to make bricks and mortar and to work long hours in the fields.

Then Pharaoh gave an order so terrible, it must have sent shock waves through the land. Work out what it was that Pharaoh said by breaking the code below. Each circle stands for a particular letter as shown.

Calling the Hebrew midwives to him, he demanded:

When you help the Hebrew women to give birth,

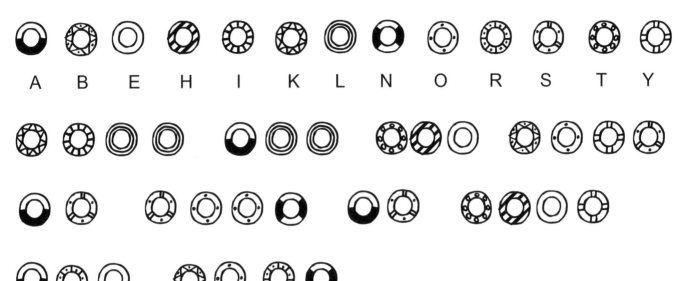

It was a shocking order, but did the midwives obey the king? Click has just printed out some more information, but some of the letters are missing. Can you help us to make sense of it by filling in the blanks?

a     e     i     o     u

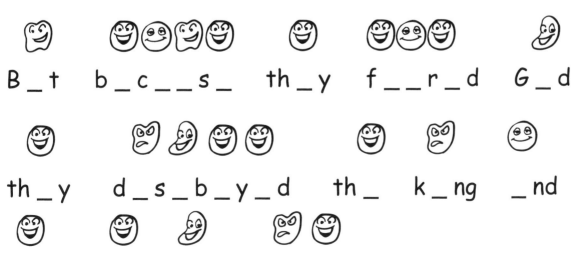

B _ t     b _ c _ _ s _     th _ y     f _ _ r _ d     G _ d

th _ y     d _ s _ b _ y _ d     th _     k _ ng     _ nd

l _ t     th _     b _ ys     l _ v _.

5

Of course, the king discovered what was happening and he wasn't pleased.

Why have you done this?

The midwives replied:

Sir, these women are very strong. Their babies arrive so quickly, we can't get here in time. They are not slow in giving birth like Egyptian women.

It was clever of the midwives to come up with these excuses and very brave of them too. God was pleased, and because these women feared him, he gave them families of their own. Meanwhile, the Israelites kept growing in number, and seeing them becoming even more powerful, Pharaoh took action. He gave another terrible order. Follow the line to reveal what it was

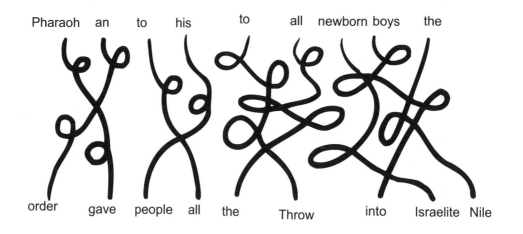

Pharaoh an to his to all newborn boys the

order gave people all the Throw into Israelite Nile

It was a shocking thing to do, and those poor slaves must have been scared stiff. Surely something had to happen! We must move on and find out.

## Study Two: The Birth of Moses

Here is an Israelite couple with a secret to hide. Amram and his wife Jochabed. What should have been a very special time for them had become a nightmare and they were worried. Perhaps you can guess what they were so desperate to keep hidden?

I'm sure you guessed, didn't you? They have a baby boy that they must keep hidden from the Egyptians. Baby Moses was a healthy baby boy with a fine set of lungs. Far too noisy to hide for long – but Moses' mother was determined that he was not going to be killed.

Taking some papyrus reeds, and some tar and pitch for waterproofing, she made a little basket. Click has printed a picture of baby Moses being lowered into the river Nile. Can you spot five differences?

Uh oh! Someone is watching baby Moses from the reeds. Count two letters back and work out whether it's friend or foe.

OQUGU' DKI UKUVGT OKTKCO

Well, that's a relief, but Moses was still in danger. We've just discovered that soon after this, one of Pharaoh's daughters came to bathe in the river. Catching sight of the basket floating there and curious to know what was inside, she called one of her servant girls to get it for her.

Inside the basket, baby Moses was crying helplessly, and at once, she guessed. "He must be one of the Hebrew children," she said. But what would she do? Miriam was still waiting patiently in the reeds. Her heart must have been thumping as she went up to the princess and spoke.

> Should I go and find one of the Hebrew women to nurse the baby for you?

What a big relief it must have been for Miriam when the princess said, "Yes, do." Moses seemed to be out of danger, and Miriam raced home joyfully to fetch her mother.

Count back two letters to find out what the princess said when Moses' mother came.

VCMG  VJKU  EJKNF  JQOG  CPF  PWTUG  JKO

HQT  OG  K  YKNN  RCA  AQW  HQT  AQWT  JGNR.

What an amazing thing to happen. And later, when Moses was older, his mother took him back to the princess, who adopted him as her son.

JESUS FACT FILE: Can you think of another amazing story about a baby who was in danger from a King? Look up Matthew chapter 2 to find out about the young child Jesus and how he had to escape to Egypt to flee from King Herod.

## Study Three: Moses escapes to Midian

So, Moses grew up. But we can't stop here. Click has just emailed us with some news of something serious – murder.

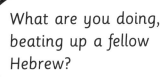

**Exodus 2:11–23**

It happened one day when Moses went out to visit his people, the Israelites. Nothing had changed, and they were being forced to work very hard. Then Moses saw an Egyptian beating one of the Hebrew slaves and something snapped. Looking around to check that no one was watching, Moses killed the Egyptian and buried him in the sand. Perhaps Moses thought he'd got away with it, because the next day, he went out to visit his people again. This time he saw two Hebrew men fighting, and he asked the one who was in the wrong,

> What are you doing, beating up a fellow Hebrew?

He must have had a shock when he heard the man's reply.

Moses was very scared. Everyone knew what he had done. What would happen if Pharaoh found out?

Sure enough, when the news did reach the king, he showed no mercy. The order went out that Moses was to be killed.

> Who made you our ruler and judge? Are you going to kill me like you killed that Egyptian yesterday?

Rather than face death, Moses fled to Midian. Follow the lines to find the way.

In Midian, there was a priest named Jethro who had seven daughters. They were shepherdesses, and it was their job to find water for the flocks. But there was a problem. When they went to the local well, the other shepherds would chase the girls and their flocks away.

Not this time, though. At watering time Moses saw what was happening and rescued the girls. Then he helped them to draw water for the flocks.

Jethro found out what had happened, and he sent the girls to invite their rescuer for a meal. Moses agreed to come, and he settled down to live with them. In time, Jethro gave one of his daughters to be Moses' wife.

9

We want to find out the name of Moses' wife, but to do that, we need to answer the following questions. Let's go for it - the vertical column will reveal her name.

1. A son of Jacob
2. They were a threat to Pharaoh
3. City built by slaves
4. Baby Moses' rescuer
5. Pharaoh issued a terrible one to the midwives
6. A sister's hiding place
7. The name of Moses' father
8. The nationality of the two fighting men.

| | | Vertical column ↓ | | | | | | | | | |
|---|---|---|---|---|---|---|---|---|---|---|---|
| 1. | | | b | | | | | | | | |
| 2. | | | r | | | l | | | | | |
| 3. | | | t | h | | | | | | | |
| 4. | | r | | | c | | | | | | |
| 5. | | r | d | | | | | | | | |
| 6. | | e | | d | | | | | | | |
| 7. | | | r | a | | | | | | | |
| 8. | | e | b | | | w | | | | | |

Let's keep going because Click has just turned up some information. It records that Moses and his wife had a baby son. Let's follow the lines and find out his name.

Meanwhile, back in Egypt, things hadn't got any better for the slaves, even though the king had died. Day after day they laboured for long hours in the sweltering heat and dust. It was exhausting work and they felt completely desperate.

But hope was not lost. You see, God heard their groans and cries for help and saw their misery and he was very concerned.

Start

## Study Four: Moses and the Burning Bush

Exodus 3: 1-22

So, what had the Hebrew slaves got to do with Moses? After all, he was far away in the safety of Midian. Well, it seems that even though Moses had run away from Egypt, God had plans for Moses to go back. Here's a picture of Moses on a seemingly ordinary day. There he was, minding his own business, looking after his father in law's flocks, when a very strange thing happened.

The place was Sinai, the mountain of God, and something very unusual had caught Moses' eye. A bush was on fire, but it wasn't burning up. "Moses, Moses!" a voice called from the bush.

"Here I am," replied Moses. Amazing! What was God going to say next? To find out, we need to arrange the numbers into the right order.

God said, "I am the God of your father, the God of Abraham, the God of Isaac and the God of Jacob." Moses was so afraid that he hid his face. God told Moses that he had seen the misery of the Israelite slaves and that he was going to rescue them. What was more, he had a special task for Moses. He was to speak to Pharaoh, then lead the slaves out of Egypt and into a new land.

11

Pretty scary, huh? Can you imagine how Moses felt? "Who am I that I should go to Pharaoh and bring the slaves out of Egypt?" he said. But this is what God replied. Place the signs in the right order but remember that there are matching pairs. The small signs below will give you a clue to the order and the first signs are numbered to give you a helping hand.

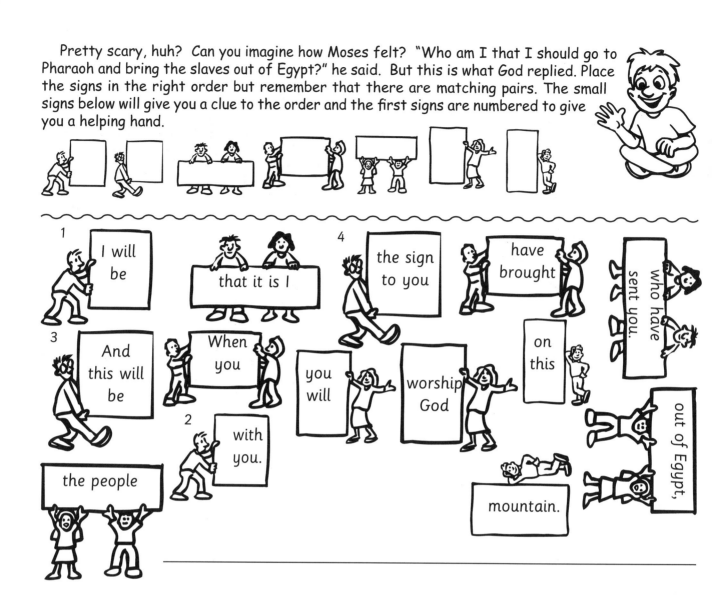

"But, what if I tell the Israelites that the God of their fathers has sent me and they ask for your name, what shall I tell them?" Moses asked. And God said, "I AM WHO I AM. Tell them that I AM has sent you to them." Then God told him to call together the leaders of Israel and give them a message.

"The Lord, the God of your fathers – the God of Abraham, Isaac and Jacob, appeared to me and said this: I have watched over you and I've seen what has been done to you in Egypt. I have promised to bring you out of your misery in Egypt and into the land of the

| | | | a | | | | | | |
|---|---|---|---|---|---|---|---|---|---|
| | | | i | | | | | | |
| | | o | | | | | | | |
| | e | | | | | | | | |
| | v | | | | | | | | |

Can you help us to put the right words into the slots? The correct words are inside the bumble bees on the next page. But there is one word that doesn't fit in the grid above - which is it?

Hittites    Amorites    Perizzites    Jebusites    Hivites    Canaanites

Here was a challenge.  Would the leaders of Israel listen to him?  God reassured Moses that they would.  The next challenge would be to get Pharaoh to take him seriously.  Let's work out what Moses had to say.  Click has printed out the beginning, but we need to take each starred letter and spell out the rest.

*"The Lord, the God of the Hebrews has met with us."*

| *L | X | Y | Z | *E | *T | X | Y | Z | *U | *S |
|----|----|----|----|----|----|----|----|----|----|----|
| *T | *A | X | Y | *K | *E | Z | *A | *T | *H | X |
| *R | *E | *E | Y | Z | X | Y | Z | *D | *A | X |
| Y | Z | *Y | *J | *O | X | Y | Z | *U | *R | *N |
| *E | *Y | X | Y | Z | *I | *N | *T | X | Y | *O |
| X | Y | *T | *H | Z | *E | *D | X | *E | *S | Y |
| Z | *E | *R | *T | *T | X | Y | *O | Z | X | Z |
| X | *O | X | Y | Z | *F | *F | *E | X | Y | Z |
| *R | X | Y | *S | Z | *A | *C | *R | X | Y | Z |
| *I | *F | X | Y | Z | X | Y | *I | *C | *E | Z |
| *S | X | Y | Z | X | Y | Z | *T | X | Y | Z |
| *O | X | Y | Z | X | *O | Z | X | Y | Z | X |
| Y | Z | *U | *R | *G | Z | X | Y | Z | *O | *D |

\_ \_ \_   \_ \_   \_ \_ \_ \_   \_   \_ \_ \_ \_ \_   \_ \_ \_   \_ \_ \_ \_ \_ \_   \_ \_ \_ \_

\_ \_ \_   \_ \_ \_ \_ \_ \_   \_ \_   \_ \_ \_ \_ \_   \_ \_ \_ \_ \_ \_ \_ \_ \_   \_ \_

\_ \_ \_   \_ \_ \_

Impossible, right?  But God was quick to reassure Moses, "Pharaoh isn't going to let you go unless he's put under heavy pressure.  So, I'm going to strike the Egyptians with many signs and wonders and then he will let you go.  I'm also going to see to it that the Egyptians treat you well.  When the Israelite women leave, their Egyptian neighbours will give them silver and gold jewellery and fine clothing."  The pace is quickening - so, let's move on and find out what happened.

## Study Five: Signs for Moses

Our research always proves that God is true to his promises, and when he asks us to do something for him, he often sends us encouragement. When Moses began to worry that no one would believe him, God used a miracle to give him confidence.

"What do you have in your hand?" God asked.

"A staff," said Moses

"Throw it on the ground," God said, and when Moses did so, his staff became a snake.

Moses was terrified, and he turned and ran! God spoke again. "Reach out and take hold of its tail," he urged. When Moses did this the snake turned back into a staff in his hand.

"If you perform this sign they will believe you," said God.

That wasn't all. God spoke again and told Moses to put his hand inside his coat. He obeyed, but when he pulled out his hand it was covered in leprosy. He did the same thing again, and the next time his hand was healthy.

> Here is a spot the difference picture to do. There are five differences for you to find.

But what if these miracles didn't persuade Pharaoh?

Well, then there were more instructions. Moses was told to take some water from the River Nile, to pour it onto the dry ground and it would turn into blood. But Moses was still worried.

"Lord, I'm no good at speaking, I'm clumsy with words."

God wasn't having any of it. "Who makes mouths?" he asked. "Who makes people deaf or unable to speak, and who makes them blind or gives them sight? Is it not I, the Lord?" Go to the next page and read the code grid and then do the puzzle to find out what else God said. Each number in the puzzle will match a letter in the code grid. Happy puzzling!

JESUS FACT FILE: Leprosy was an incurable skin disease. If you look up Matthew chapter 8 you can read about how Jesus healed a leper. God has power over sickness and disease. Jesus showed this power. He has power over death. He conquered death when he came back to life three days after he was killed on the cross. You can read about this story in John chapters 19-20.

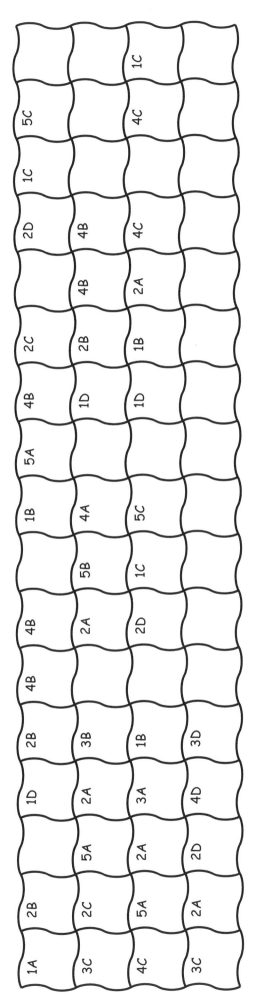

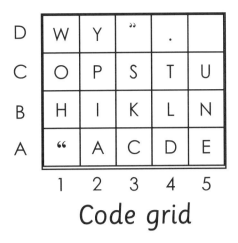

### Code grid

So, was Moses full of faith and ready for anything? Well, no. He still wasn't sure and pleaded with God to send someone else to do it.

God was angry. However, he gave permission for Aaron, Moses' brother to speak on his behalf.

To find out what God said look at the picture clues underneath the palm tree. Fill in the gaps by writing down the initial letter of each object.

God said, "_ _ _ _ _ will _ _ _ _ _ to the people for you, and it will be as if he were your _ _ _ _ _, and as if you were God to him. But take your _ _ _ _ _ with you so that you can perform miraculous _ _ _ _ _ with it."

## Study Six: Back to Egypt

It was time to move on. God had told Moses that all the men who wanted to kill him were dead. So Moses went to Jethro and asked if he could go back to Egypt and find out if any member of his family was still alive.

"Go with my blessing," Jethro said, and preparations began for the journey back with his wife and sons.

It wasn't going to be easy and God warned Moses that even though he would perform all the wonders he had given him to do, it would not persuade Pharaoh. The King of Egypt's heart would be hard and he would not let the people go.

We've uncovered the message that Moses had to give Pharaoh, but there are some gaps. Let's see if we can piece it together using the clock puzzle below.

8am,6pm,5pm,12am,4am,11am

5am,8am,5pm,6pm,7pm,1am,2pm,5pm,1pm   6pm,2pm,1pm

2am,2pm,12pm,12pm,12am,1pm,3am,4am,3am        10pm,2pm,5pm,6pm,7am,8am,3pm

_ _ _ _ _ _ is my _ _ _ _ _ _ _ _ _ _ _ _ _. I _ _ _ _ _ _ _ _ _ _ you to let him

go so he could _ _ _ _ _ _ _ me. But as you refused to let him go, I will kill your

firstborn son.

Meanwhile, back in Egypt, God was speaking to Aaron, but what exactly did he say? We need to follow the wiggly lines to find out.

1. Go to Pharaoh and tell him to let the Israelites go.

2. Go to Pharaoh's Palace and wait for Moses.

3. Go into the desert to meet Moses.

AARON

Aaron obeyed God, and went out to meet Moses, greeting him warmly. Then Moses explained everything. Together, they returned to Egypt to meet with the Israelite leaders. Let's continue our detective work to find out how they reacted. Take the first letter of each object to work out what happened next.

## Study Seven:  Bricks without straw

You might be wondering what a stack of bricks and a pile of straw have to do with the story.  Well, we've been finding out! First, let's see what happened when Moses and Aaron went to call on Pharaoh.

Remember that Moses and Aaron had to ask Pharaoh for three days off so that they could hold a festival in God's honour. It must have been pretty scary to go before the most powerful man in Egypt with such a request. And it didn't take a rocket scientist to work out his reply. Let's see if you can. Click has downloaded a puzzle for you to work out. Pharaoh's words have been encripted. Can you break the code?

A   B   E   H   I   K   L   N   O   R   S   T   W

_ h _    _ _    _ _ _    _ _ _ d    _ _ _ _    _

_ _ _ u _ d    _ _ _ y    _ _ m    _ _ d    _ _ _

_ _ _ _ _ _    g _ ?    _    d    _    _ _ _

_ _ _ _    _ _ _    _ _ _ d    _ _ d

_    _ _ _ _    _ _ _    _ _ _    _ _ _ _ _    g _ .

Moses and Aaron didn't give up.  "If we don't go, God might strike us down with diseases or with the sword," they insisted, but the king was unmoved.  "These people are lazy," he declared to the slave drivers.  "Make them get their own straw for making bricks.  Tell them to make the same number of bricks as before."  It was bad news.  Of course, the Israelites couldn't make as many bricks.  The foremen in charge of the crews treated them brutally.  The Israelites were angry and blamed Moses and Aaron.  What would happen now?

## Study Eight: Promises of Deliverance

Can you guess how Moses felt as he turned to God for answers? But it was all a part of God's plan. "Now see what I will do to Pharaoh," he said. "When he feels my hand upon him, he'll be so keen to get rid of my people, he'll force them to leave." And God made a wonderful promise to the Israelites. Can you work it out?

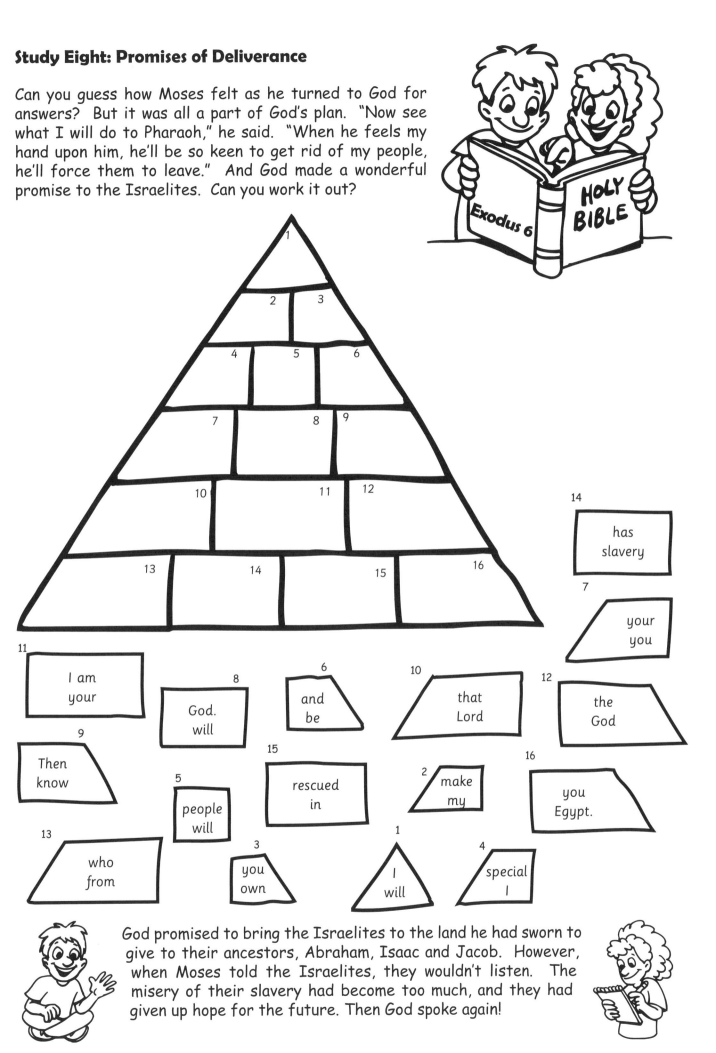

Exodus 6

HOLY BIBLE

14
has slavery

7
your you

11
I am your

8
God. will

6
and be

10
that Lord

12
the God

9
Then know

5
people will

15
rescued in

2
make my

16
you Egypt.

13
who from

3
you own

1
I will

4
special I

God promised to bring the Israelites to the land he had sworn to give to their ancestors, Abraham, Isaac and Jacob. However, when Moses told the Israelites, they wouldn't listen. The misery of their slavery had become too much, and they had given up hope for the future. Then God spoke again!

19

## Study Nine: Aaron's staff becomes a snake

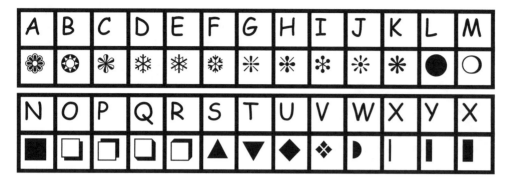

"Go back to Pharaoh," said God. "And tell him to let my people go." Moses remembered the last time. "I can't do it God. I'm no good at speaking. Why would Pharaoh listen to me?"
"Your brother Aaron will speak for you," God said, "You just tell him what to say. I will make Pharaoh stubborn and he won't listen to you. Then I will cause disasters to fall on Egypt and before long, they will realise that I am God.

| A | B | C | D | E | F | G | H | I | J | K | L | M |
|---|---|---|---|---|---|---|---|---|---|---|---|---|
| ✺ | ◉ | ✳ | ❄ | ❅ | ❆ | ✴ | ✳ | ❉ | ❋ | ✶ | ● | ○ |

| N | O | P | Q | R | S | T | U | V | W | X | Y | X |
|---|---|---|---|---|---|---|---|---|---|---|---|---|
| ■ | □ | ◻ | ◻ | ◻ | ▲ | ▼ | ◆ | ❖ | ◗ | ▮ | ▯ | ▮ |

Pharaoh was probably very annoyed with these tiresome Israelites. He was, after all the most powerful man in Egypt. There was no way he was going to give in to their demands! But remember that God had prepared Moses and Aaron with something to make Pharaoh sit up and take notice. Siezing his moment, Aaron threw down his staff in front of the king and his officials and it turned into a slithering snake.

But, just as God had warned, Pharaoh wasn't impressed. He called together his magicians, sorcerers and wise men and they set to work with their magic arts. They threw down their staffs, and soon they, too, had created a mass of writhing snakes.

Ughh! I'm glad I wasn't there, aren't you? But had it all been a waste of time? Let's find out what happened next.

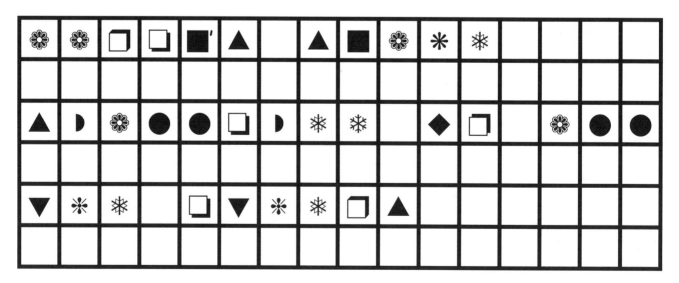

Did it make any difference? Well, no - Pharaoh's heart stayed hard and he still refused to listen. But this was only the beginning; let's crack on now and find out what happened next.

## Study Ten: The Plague of Blood

Click has downloaded a copy of some fresh instructions, which God gave Moses, but some of the words have got mixed up. Can you unjumble them and find out what Moses had to do.

Exodus 7:14-24

HOLY BIBLE

In the gronmin go to the virer Neil with your fafts and wait for harPhoa to come.

Something terrible was going to happen, which would prove that God was the Lord. God said to Moses, "Tell Aaron, 'take your staff and stretch it over the waters of Egypt – over the streams and canals, over the ponds and all the reservoirs, and they will turn into blood. There will be blood everywhere – even in the wooden buckets and stone jars in people's homes.'"

Click has printed out a wordsearch for us. Can you find the following?

| streams | ponds | reservoirs | buckets | Nile |
|---------|-------|------------|---------|------|
| jars | blood | staff | water | canals |

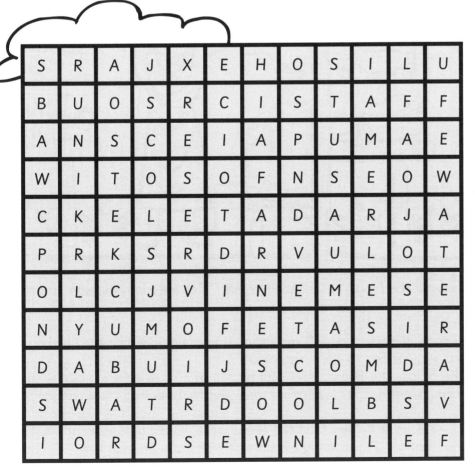

| S | R | A | J | X | E | H | O | S | I | L | U |
|---|---|---|---|---|---|---|---|---|---|---|---|
| B | U | O | S | R | C | I | S | T | A | F | F |
| A | N | S | C | E | I | A | P | U | M | A | E |
| W | I | T | O | S | O | F | N | S | E | O | W |
| C | K | E | L | E | T | A | D | A | R | J | A |
| P | R | K | S | R | D | R | V | U | L | O | T |
| O | L | C | J | V | I | N | E | M | E | S | E |
| N | Y | U | M | O | F | E | T | A | S | I | R |
| D | A | B | U | I | J | S | C | O | M | D | A |
| S | W | A | T | R | D | O | O | L | B | S | V |
| I | O | R | D | S | E | W | N | I | L | E | F |

Moses and Aaron followed God's instructions and everything happened exactly as God had said. There was blood all over the place. The fish died and the river smelled so bad, the Egyptians couldn't drink the water. It seems that the magicians could do the same thing, though. Pharaoh, unmoved by all that was happening, stalked off back to the palace.

## Study Eleven: The Plague of Frogs

Exodus 8: 1-15

Well, detectives, Pharaoh was becoming even more stubborn. One week later Moses and Aaron were back at the palace again, and the message was the same.

God says, 'Let my people go so that they can worship me. If you don't, I will send a plague of frogs across your land.'

"They will come into your houses, into your bedrooms and even into your beds. They'll find their way into your ovens and your kneading bowls. You will be overwhelmed by them."

But, surprise, surprise, Pharaoh refused! Aaron stretched out his staff over the waters of Egypt and the frog invasion began. Can you picture the chaos as millions of the little creatures crawled through the land, hopping into houses and finding their way into all the nooks and crannies? And, of course, not to be outdone, the magicians set to work creating even more.

It was too much for Pharaoh, and summoning Moses and Aaron, he begged them to take away the frogs. "I'll let the people go so that they can offer sacrifices to the Lord," he promised, "just plead with God to get rid of these pests!"

Look at these two spot the difference pictures. There are five for you to find.

Moses agreed to ask God to remove the frogs. He asked Pharaoh, "Tell me when you want me to pray for the frogs to go."

"Tomorrow," replied Pharaoh.

"Right," said Moses. "I will do it, and then you will know that there is no-one like the Lord our God. All the frogs will be destroyed, except for those in the river."

Moses prayed, and soon the fields, the houses and courtyards of Egypt were strewn with dead frogs. The people piled them into great heaps, and before long, the foul smell of their rotting bodies filled the land.

Revolting! But guess what? As soon as he saw that the frogs were dead, Pharaoh went back on his word and wouldn't let the Israelites go. It was a big mistake of his – let's find out why.

## Study Twelve: Gnats and Flies

God said to Moses, "Tell Aaron to strike the dust on the ground with his staff." Aaron obeyed and great swarms of gnats began to infest the land, covering the Egyptians and their animals. This time, when the magicians tried to produce gnats, they found it impossible. Click has printed a puzzle, which will reveal what they said.

Pharaoh refused to change his mind, and soon another plague hit Egypt. But just to show Pharaoh that God was looking after his people, this one only affected the Egyptians. What was it? Look at the back to front writing and see if you can work it out.

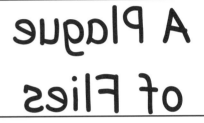

A Plague of Flies

These little creatures were everywhere - crawling in the food, and on people's faces, swarming around animals and buzzing noisily. It was so bad that Pharaoh gave in - but only a little. "You can offer the sacrifices," he said, "but only here in this land."

"That's not good enough," Moses replied. "The Egyptians would detest our sacrifices and they would stone us. We must make a three-day journey into the wilderness as God commanded."

"All right," said Pharaoh. "You can go into the desert and offer sacrifices, but don't go far. Now, pray for me." Moses left Pharaoh with the promise that he would pray, but he also left with a warning.

The next day all the flies disappeared. Pharaoh, however, was not true to his word and would not let the people go.

## Study Thirteen: Cattle, Boils and Hail

The plagues kept coming. All the Egyptian horses, camels, sheep, goats and donkeys were wiped out, but no animal belonging to an Israelite died. Then, when Pharaoh refused to change his mind, God told Moses to throw soot into the air.

**Exodus 9:1-35**

As Pharaoh watched, terrible boils broke out on the Egyptians and their animals. Even the magicians couldn't stand before Moses because boils had broken out on them too. Still Pharaoh refused to change.

Can you spot five differences in the following two pictures?

We reckon that lots of people would have given in by now, but not Pharaoh. The next message from God should have had him shaking in his shoes.

God then said, "I could have sent a plague that would have wiped you from the face of the earth, but I have allowed you to live for this reason..." Match the pieces and find out what.

God says, 'Let my people go so they can worship me. If you don't, I will send a plague that will really speak to you.'

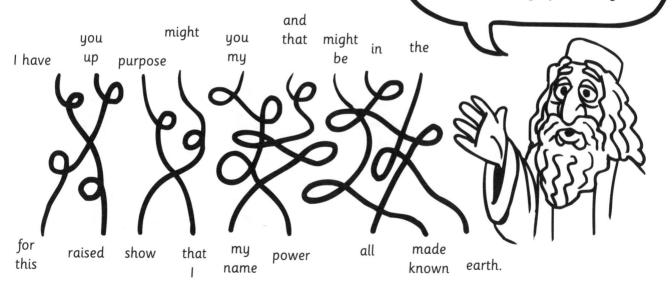

I have  you  might  you  and  that  might  in  the
up  purpose  my  be

for  raised  show  that  my  power  all  made  earth.
this  I  name  known

God told Pharaoh that the next day he would send the worst hailstorm that Egypt had ever known. He told Pharaoh to order every person and animal in from the fields or they would die. When the message was delivered, all the Egyptians who feared God rushed to bring their servants and livestock in from the fields. But some chose not to and left them out in the open. The next day God told Moses to stretch his hand out to the sky, and when he did, thunder, hail and lightning struck the land. In all of Egypt's history, there had never been a storm like it. Everything that had been left in the fields was destroyed – men, animals and crops. Even the trees were stripped bare.

There was only one place where it didn't hail. Let's get Click to help us with our investigations. If we answer the questions Click's printed, we can find out where it was.

1.    "This is the _ _ _ _ _ _ of God," the magicians said after one of the plagues.

2.    The Egyptians found frogs in them.

3.    One of the plagues.

4.    The number of days needed by the Israelites to worship God in the desert.

5.    The only place where the frogs didn't die.

6.    An Egyptian river.

Of course this was the place where the Israelites lived. Once again, God was showing Pharaoh that he was protecting his people. So, what happened next?

Look at this column ↓

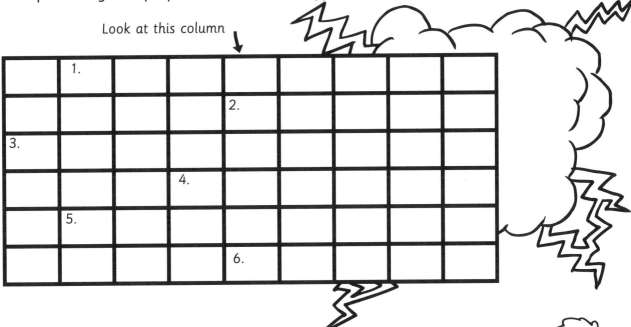

Well, Pharaoh summoned Moses again and asked him to beg God to stop the thunder and hail. "This time I will let you go," he said, but it was a hollow promise. As soon as the weather got better, he broke his word and refused to let the Israelites go – just as God had predicted.

## Study Fourteen: A Plague of Locusts

What a stubborn, hard-hearted man Pharaoh was – although the Bible says that it was God who made him that way. God did this so that he could perform all these miraculous signs then the Israelites could tell their children and grandchildren about them. So, the plagues kept coming. Once again, Moses came before Pharaoh and told him what would happen if he didn't let the Israelites go. Let's work out what it would be. The code grid here is all that you need to work out what the word is below. Once you have worked it out write the correct word inside this box.

C L | O S
• | •
—————+—————
T | U

"There will be so many of them that you won't be able to see the ground," Moses told Pharaoh. "They will eat everything that escaped the hailstorm and they will fill your houses and palaces." Then he walked out of the palace.

By now, the court officials were getting worried. "How long will these disasters go on?" they asked. "Why don't you let them go and worship their God. Don't you realise that Egypt is ruined?" So, Moses and Aaron were brought back to Pharaoh.

"You can go and worship your God," he said. "but who are you taking with you?"

"All of us will go," replied Moses "and our flocks and herds. We must all be there to celebrate the festival to the Lord."

"Never." Pharaoh replied. "I can see right through your wicked plans. Only the men may go." And at that, Moses and Aaron were thrown out of the palace.

God told Moses to lift his staff over Egypt, and an east wind blew for the rest of the day and night. By morning, the worst plague of locusts in Egyptian history arrived. Anything left after the hailstorm was gobbled up, and soon, not even a blade of grass could be found. A worried Pharaoh assured Moses that he would let the people go. How did God get rid of the locusts? Break the code to find out.

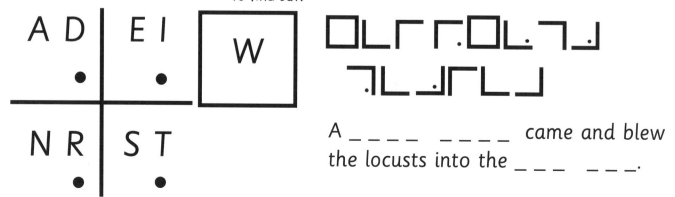

A _ _ _ _  _ _ _ _ came and blew the locusts into the _ _ _  _ _ _.

Once again the danger had passed, and once again Pharaoh broke his word. The next plague to hit the land was terrifying.

26

## Study Fifteen: A Plague of Darkness

A deep darkness fell over the land. No one could see anyone else, and the people could hardly move because of it. In Goshen, though, the Israelites went about their business in daylight, as usual. Soon, Moses and Aaron found themselves back in the palace.

Exodus 10:21-29

HOLY BIBLE

You can go and worship the Lord and you can even take your children. But you are to leave your flocks and herds here.

"Oh, no," said Moses. "Everything must go with us. You see, we will have to choose our sacrifices from among these animals and we won't know which ones God will require until we get there."

Pharaoh was very angry. "Get out of here," he shouted at Moses. "I don't ever want to see you again. The day you do, you will die!"

"Very well," replied Moses. "I will never see you again." But there was still one more plague to come – something so terrible, it would never be forgotten. But first, let's see how much we can remember!

# Master Detective Quiz

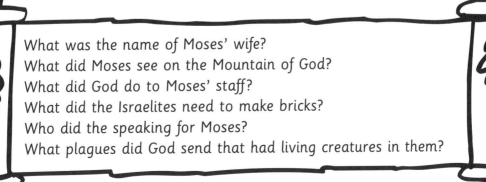

How many books are in the Old Testament?
Who forgave his brothers for selling him into slavery?
Name the two cities the Israelite slaves built?
Who did Pharaoh order to kill the newly born Israelite baby boys?
Who were Moses' mum and dad?
Why did Moses have to run away?
Where did he run away to?

What was the name of Moses' wife?
What did Moses see on the Mountain of God?
What did God do to Moses' staff?
What did the Israelites need to make bricks?
Who did the speaking for Moses?
What plagues did God send that had living creatures in them?

## Study Sixteen: The Firstborn Plague

So it was now time for the final plague – and God left Moses in no doubt about the result. "After this, Pharaoh will be so anxious for you to go, he will almost drive you out," he said. Then he gave Moses some instructions, and because the Egyptians looked favourably upon the Israelites and Moses, they did as they were asked. What was it? Take the words from the treasure chest and put them in the right order in the shapes below.

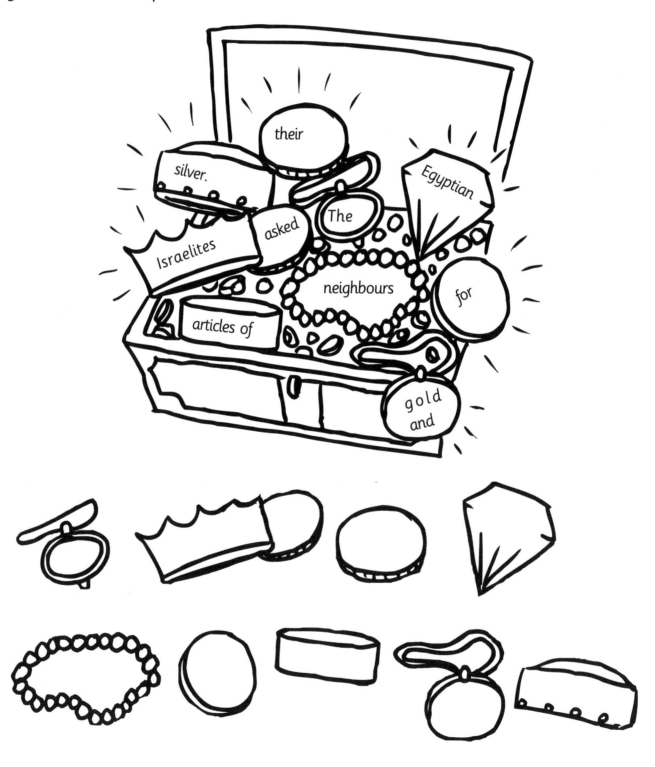

Then Moses made an announcement to Pharaoh. Let's find out what he said by reading around the circles and wiggily lines.

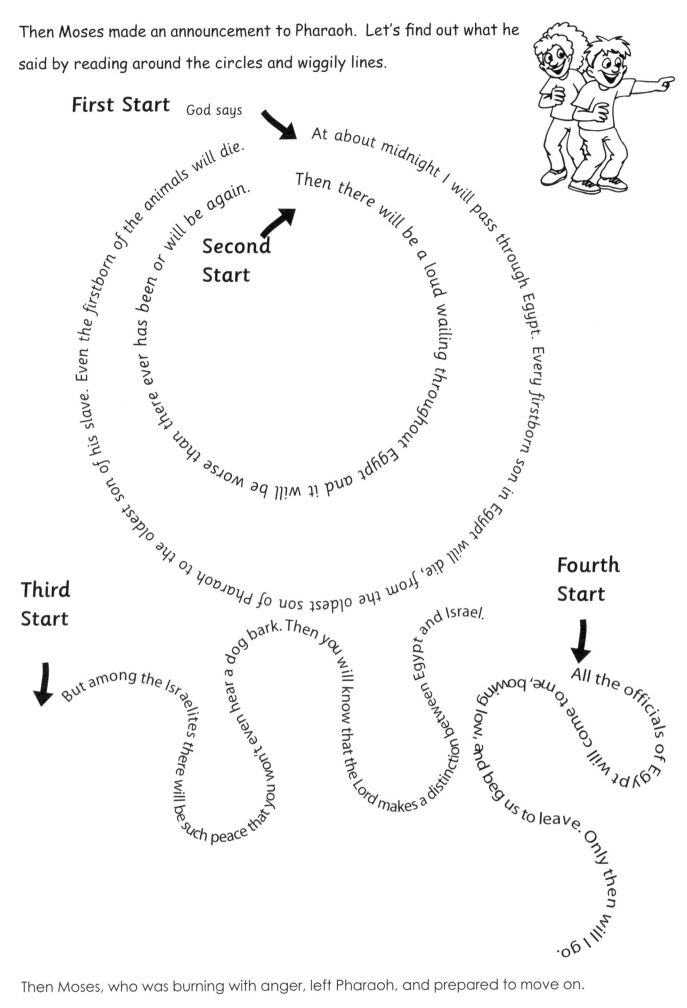

**First Start** God says

At about midnight I will pass through Egypt. Every firstborn son in Egypt will die, from the oldest son of Pharaoh to the oldest son of his slave. Even the firstborn of the animals will die.

**Second Start** Then there will be a loud wailing throughout Egypt and it will be worse than there ever has been or will be again.

**Third Start** But among the Israelites there will be such peace that you won't even hear a dog bark. Then you will know that the Lord makes a distinction between Egypt and Israel.

**Fourth Start** All the officials of Egypt will come to me, bowing low, and beg us to leave. Only then will I go.

Then Moses, who was burning with anger, left Pharaoh, and prepared to move on.

## Study Seventeen:  The First Passover

Click has just printed out the instructions that God gave to Moses as well as another fact box about The Passover.

**Exodus 12**

From now on this month will be the first month of the year for you.

Tell all Israel that on the 10th day of this month, each family must take a year old lamb or goat without defects and sacrifice it.

If a family is too small to eat a whole lamb, let them share it with another family.

At twilight on the 14th day of the month - kill the animal. Take some blood and put it on the sides and tops of the door frames of the houses where you eat the lambs.

That night, eat the meat roasted over the fire, along with bitter herbs and bread made without yeast. If any is left over, you must burn it.

You must eat it with your cloak tucked into your belt, your sandals on your feet and your staff in your hand. Eat it quickly - it is the Lord's Passover.

### JESUS FACT FILE:

The Passover was the special meal that Jesus celebrated with his disciples just before he was killed on the cross.

During that meal Jesus broke some bread to show how his body would be broken. The wine was poured to show how he would bleed.

Jesus had to go through all this to save his people from their sins.

The Passover meal reminded God's people about how they were rescued from Egypt. Today Christians have a special meal of bread and wine to remind them of Jesus' love for them.

The Israelites did all that God had commanded.  At midnight, God killed all the firstborn sons in Egypt, and the firstborn of the livestock.  The only people who were spared, were those who had blood on the top and sides of their doorframes. Pharaoh and his officials and all the Egyptians got up during the night, for there wasn't a single house where someone had not died. Moses and Aaron were called to the palace for the last time.  What did Pharaoh say to them? Break the code to find out the answer.

Go away! _ _ _ _ _ us, all of you.  Go and _ _ _ _ _ _ _ the

Lord.  Take your _ _ _ _ _ _ and _ _ _ _ _ and give  me a

_ _ _ _ _ _ _ _ .

The Egyptians couldn't get rid of the Israelites fast enough. You see, they thought that they would all die. They even gave them articles of silver and gold when asked, just as God had said. That night, 600,000 men, plus women and children and others who were not Israelites left Egypt.  They also took with them, the bones of their ancestor Joseph.  And every year from that day on, Passover has been celebrated. So now that the Israelites had a journey to start how did they know which way to go?

Good question, Harry.  Let's find out.

| Q 1 | W 2 | E 3 | R 4 | T 5 | Y 6 | U 7 | I 8 | O 9 | P 10 |
| A 11 | S 12 | D 13 | F 14 | G 15 | H 16 | J 17 | K 18 | L 19 | ' 20 |
| Z 21 | X 22 | C 23 | V 24 | B 25 | N 26 | M 27 | , 28 | . 29 | / 30 |

SPACE
31

They followed a pillar of 14,8,4,3        11,5        26,8,15,16,5

and a pillar of 23, 19, 9, 7, 13        25,6        13,11,6

## Study Eighteen: The Egyptians pursue Israel

Exodus 14

Meanwhile, back at Pharaoh's palace, he and his officials were regretting their actions. It was clear that the Israelites were not going to come back and they were not pleased. "What have we done?" they said, "We've let our slaves get away." It was time to take action, and Pharaoh gave orders to make his chariot ready. Then, taking all his horses, chariots, horsemen and troops, he set off in hot pursuit.

Perhaps it was the sound of the thundering hooves or the rumbling of the chariots that made the Israelites look anxiously behind. In the distance there was a large cloud of dust. The entire Egyptian army was chasing them. It was terrifying – and even more so, when they realised that they were trapped. In front of them flowed the waters of the Red Sea, and it was impossible to get across. What would they do now? Let's find out what Moses said to them.

Unscramble the words and fit them into the right places.

Don't be _ _ _ _ _ _. Stay where you are because _ _ _ _ _ God will _ _ _ _ _ _ you. The Egyptians you see _ _ _ _ _ you will _ _ _ _ _ _ see again. The Lord will _ _ _ _ _ for you. Just be _ _ _ _ _.

dafira

yodta

ecruse

yodta

vrene

tifhg

listl

32

# Study Ninteen: Escape through the Red Sea

Click has just downloaded a code for us to work on. It will tell us what God told Moses to do. Turn this page on its side to view the key and puzzle.

Exodus 14:15-31

Red Sea Escape

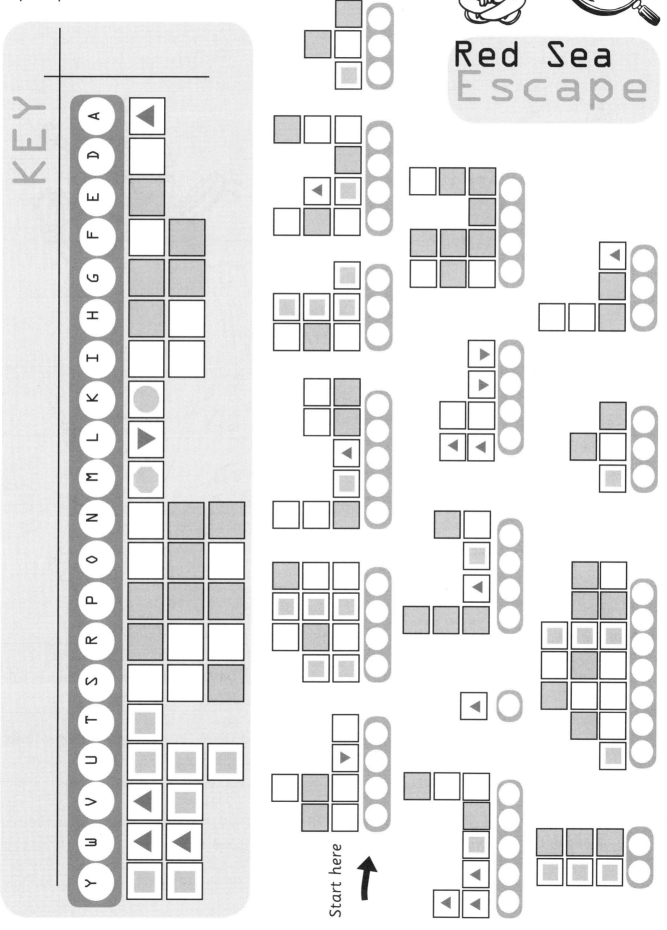

Start here

Meanwhile, the angel of God who had been travelling in front of the Israelites, moved behind them. The pillar of cloud also moved behind them and settled between the Israelite and Egyptian camps. Night-time came and the pillar of cloud became a pillar of fire, which lit the Israelite camp. But the cloud brought darkness to the Egyptians and they couldn't find the Israelites.

Then Moses stretched out his hand over the sea and God opened up a path through the water.

Can you match the words to the pictures? Write the correct number to match the picture.

1. A strong east wind blew during the night and the seabed turned into dry land.

2. The people of Israel walked through the sea on dry ground, with a wall of water on either side of them.

3. The Egyptians with their horses and chariots followed them, but early in the morning, God threw their army into confusion. Their chariot wheels came off so that they couldn't drive. "Let's get away from here," they cried. "The Lord is fighting against us."

4. Once the Israelites had reached the other side, God told Moses to raise his hand over the sea again. As he did so, the water roared back, covering Pharaoh's army.

5. And when the Israelites saw God's great power displayed against the Egyptians, they feared him and put their trust in him and in Moses.

## Study Twenty: Bitter Water

You can imagine how relieved the Israelites felt. How they sang, thanking God for his power which had saved them. Then Miriam the prophet, who was Moses and Aaron's sister, took a particular instrument and led the women in dancing and singing. Can you join the dots to find out what musical instrument it was?

**Exodus 15: 22-27**

Leading the Israelites away from the Red Sea, Moses took them into the Desert of Shur. It was hot and dusty, and after three days without water, the people's spirits were sinking. They felt weary and irritable, and needed someone to blame. How could they survive without something to drink, and what about the animals? Then, just when they discovered water, it was found to be bitter and undrinkable. "What are we going to do now?" they grumbled,

Moses cried out to God for help, and the Lord showed him a piece of wood. He threw it into the water and suddenly, it became sweet. Click has emailed us a puzzle, to reveal the name of the place where it happened. Can you help?

1. A prophetess.
2. A wind which divided the Red Sea.
3. The Israelites did this when they found bitter water.
4. The women did this after the victory.
5. A desert.
It was after this that God made a promise to the Israelites.

| ↓ Where it happened | | | | | | |
|---|---|---|---|---|---|---|
| 1. | | | | | | |
| 2. | | | | | | |
| 3. | | | | | | |
| 4. | | | | | | |
| 5. | | | | | | |

Can you fill in the gaps?

If you _ _ _ _ _ _ carefully to the Lord your

God and do what is _ _ _ _ _ in his _ _ _ _ _,

if you obey his _ _ _ _ _ _ _ _ and

_ _ _ _ then I will not make you suffer the

_ _ _ _ _ _ _ _ _ I sent on the Egyptians, for

I am the Lord who _ _ _ _ _ you.

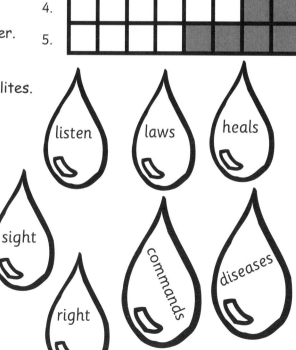

listen  laws  heals

sight

right  commands  diseases

35

## Study Twenty-One: Manna and Quail

About a month after leaving Egypt, the Israelites began to grumble again against Moses and Aaron. Can you match up the different pieces of conversation? Click has told me that the first one is Number 1 and Number 7. Now try the rest.

**Exodus 16**

1 I wish we'd stayed in

It would have been better if the Lord had 2

Yes, at least we had lots 3

to eat there. 5

Now you've brought us into the desert to 4

starve to death 6

7 Egypt.

killed us there. 8

After all these complaints Moses and Aaron called a meeting of the Israelite people.

In the evening you will realise that it was God who brought you out of Egypt. And in the morning you will see the glory of the Lord, because he has heard your grumbling against him.

Then they said

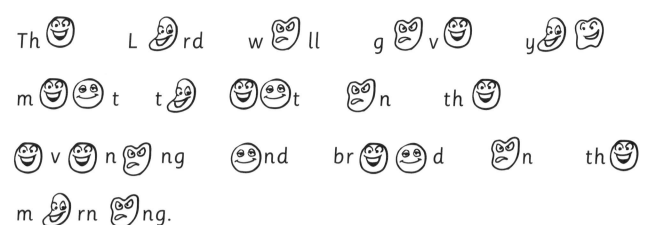

The key for this puzzle is on page five if you need some help.

While Aaron was speaking to the people, they looked towards the desert and saw the glory of God coming in the cloud. Then God said to Moses, "I have heard the Israelites complaining. Tell them that in the evening they will have meat to eat, and in the morning they will have bread. Then they will know that I am God."

That evening quail came and covered the camp, and the following morning, the desert all around the camp was covered in dew. When it was gone, thin, white flakes like frost covered the ground. "What is it?" The people asked. They had never seen it before and were really puzzled. Moses explained...

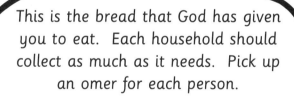

This is the bread that God has given you to eat. Each household should collect as much as it needs. Pick up an omer for each person.

Click's fact file:

Quail are small birds belonging to the partridge family.

An omer is just over 2 litres.

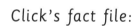

 Here are two pictures of the Israelite people collecting God's special food. Can you spot five differences in these two pictures? The people went out and gathered the food, and by following God's instructions, everyone had enough. Then Moses told them, "don't keep any of the manna overnight." Of course, some of them were disobedient and kept manna until the morning. They had a shock when they woke up, though, and it certainly made Moses very angry. What had happened?

It was

maggots and

began

full of

to smell

Each morning the food kept coming, but as the sun became hot, it melted and disappeared. On the 6th day there was twice as much on the ground, so the leaders came and asked Moses why this had happened. This is what he said.

This time, when they saved it till morning it didn't stink or get maggots in it. And those who hadn't obeyed and went out to gather food on the Sabbath found that there was nothing. From then on, the people gathered food for six days, but on the seventh there was nothing on the ground.

God has commanded that tomorrow should be a day of rest, a holy Sabbath to the Lord. So bake and boil as much as you want today, and save what is left for tomorrow.

In time, the food became known as manna. It was white, like coriander seed and tasted like wafers made with honey. Moses gave a command from God. To find out what this was break the code. Every number represents a letter. The number 1 = A and the number 2 = b and so on. See how you do.

Get a

| 10 | |
| 1 | |
| 18 | |

and put an

| 15 | |
| 13 | |
| 5 | |
| 18 | |

of

| 13 | |
| 1 | |
| 14 | |
| 14 | |
| 1 | |

into it.
Then store
it in a

| 19 | |
| 1 | |
| 3 | |
| 18 | |
| 5 | |
| 4 | |

| 16 | |
| 12 | |
| 1 | |
| 3 | |
| 5 | |

as a

| 18 | |
| 5 | |
| 13 | |
| 9 | |
| 14 | |
| 4 | |
| 5 | |
| 18 | |

for all
future

| 7 | |
| 5 | |
| 14 | |
| 5 | |
| 18 | |
| 1 | |
| 20 | |
| 9 | |
| 15 | |
| 14 | |
| 19 | |

## Study Twenty-Two: Water from the Rock

It wasn't too long before the Israelites were complaining again. They had reached a place called Rephidim, and once again there wasn't any water for them to drink.

They were very quick to forget that God had provided water for them before, weren't they? Moses was displeased. "Why are you arguing with me, and why are you testing the Lord?" he asked, but they were thirsty and went on grumbling. "Why did you bring us here?" they moaned. "We are all going to die now."

Moses turned to God. "What shall I do with these people?" He cried out to him. "They are almost ready to stone me." So God said, "Take the staff you used to strike the Nile, then call some of the elders and walk ahead of the people. I will meet you at the rock at Sinai. Strike the rock and drinking water will come pouring out of it.

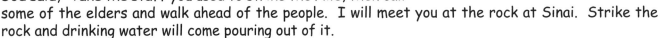

Work out the maze and help Moses and the elders find their way to the rock

Moses did as God had instructed, and soon there was plenty of water for the people to drink. Click has printed out a puzzle. Can you work out the name of the place where water was found?

## Study Twenty-Three: Israel Defeats the Amalekites

**Exodus 17:8-1 6**

Well, detectives, we're discovering that leaving Egypt was only the beginning of the adventure. As fast as one problem was sorted, another came up. Now we've uncovered some more information, which reveals that fresh trouble was brewing. The local tribes didn't like the Israelites wandering around in their area. It was too much of a threat, and they were determined to do something about it. Some warriors from a place called Amalek attacked the Israelites. Let's press on and find out what happened.

Choose some of our men and go and fight the Amalekites. Tomorrow, I will stand at the top of the hill with the staff of God in my hands.

Moses called a man named Joshua to him and issued him with some instructions.

Joshua went out to fight, and Moses, Aaron and Hur went to the top of the hill. As long as Moses held up his hands the Israelites were winning, but when he lowered them, the Amalekites began to win. As the hours passed, Moses began to grow weary. His arms must have felt like lead, but still the battle raged.

Aaron and Hur found a stone for him to sit on. Then they stood on either side of him, holding up his aching arms until sunset.

Joshua and his troops were able to defeat the Amalekites, and with a thankful heart, Moses built an altar there and called it, "The Lord is my banner."

Draw a line from the empty spaces to the missing objects or copy the objects into the picture by yourself and colour it in.

## Study Twenty-Four: Jethro's Visit to Moses

Can you remember the names of Moses' wife and two sons? Hold up a mirror to the words below and refresh your memory.

Zipporah

Gershom

Eliezer

Some time earlier, Moses had sent his wife and sons to live with his father in law, Jethro. But when Jethro heard about all the amazing things which had happened, he came with Zipporah and his grandsons to visit Moses.

Jethro was warmly welcomed, and soon Moses was telling him about everything that had happened and how God had saved them.

"Praise be to the Lord," Jethro cried with delight. We'd like to know more, and Click has helped us by printing out some information for us to work on. Fill in the following letters in their grid references.

A: a11, c1, c7, c9
D: b7, d7
E: b3, b12, c3, d3
G: b10, d5
H: a10, b2, c6, d2
I: a4, b8
K: a5

L: b4, c10, c11
N: a1, a6, c8
O: a2, a7, b5, c12, d6
R: b6, b11, c4, d4
S: b9, d8
T: a9, a12, b1, c2, c5, d1
W: a3, a8

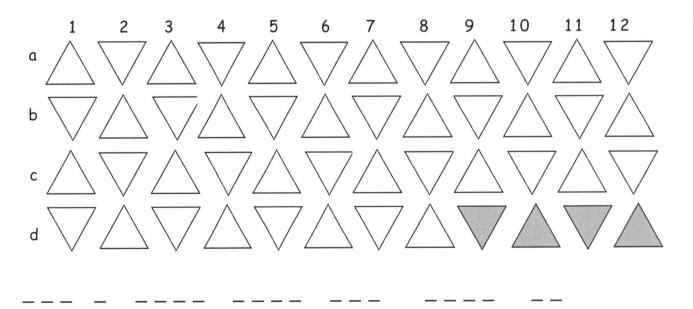

_ _ _   _   _ _ _ _   _ _ _   _ _ _ _   _ _

_ _ _ _ _ _   _ _ _   _ _   _ _ _ _   _ _ _ _ .

## Study Twenty-Five: Jethro's Wise Advice

**Exodus 18: 13-27**

It didn't take long for wise Jethro to see that Moses was overloaded with work. For one thing, he had to listen to everyone's squabbles and complaints against each other and tell them what to do. This took hours each day and was exhausting. "Why are you trying to do all this alone?" said Jethro. "The people have been waiting here for your help all day."

"The people come to me to ask for the Lord's guidance," said Moses. "I tell the people God's decisions and teach them his laws."

"This is just too much for you to do all by yourself," said Jethro, and he gave him some advice.

Look out for the highlighted letters and rearrange them. These will help you fill in the last words of Jethro's story.

You s**h**ould still be the **p**eople's representative before God and bring him their qu**e**stions to be decided.

Tell them God's decisions and te**a**ch them God's laws and instru**c**tions and show them the way to liv**e**.

Then Jethro said

Find s**o**me capable, honest men who fear God and hate bribes

Make them judg**e**s over groups of 1000, 100, 50 and 10

If you do this, and God directs you to do it, you will be able to cope with the pressures and these people will go — — — — — — — — — —

These **m**en can sort out all the ordinary cases, but anyth**i**ng too important or complicated ca**n** be brought to you.

Moses listened to the advice and saw that it made sense. He did everything that Jethro had said and things improved. Soon after this, His father in law said goodbye and returned to his own country.

43

## Study Twenty-Six: At Mount Sinai

Two months after leaving Egypt, the Israelites arrived at the base of Mount Sinai and set up camp. Moses went up the mountain to meet with God, and while he was there, God gave some instructions for the Israelites.

"You have seen what I did to Egypt and how I carried you on eagle's wings and brought you to myself ..."

Then God made an offer. Let's discover what it was.

**Exodus 19**

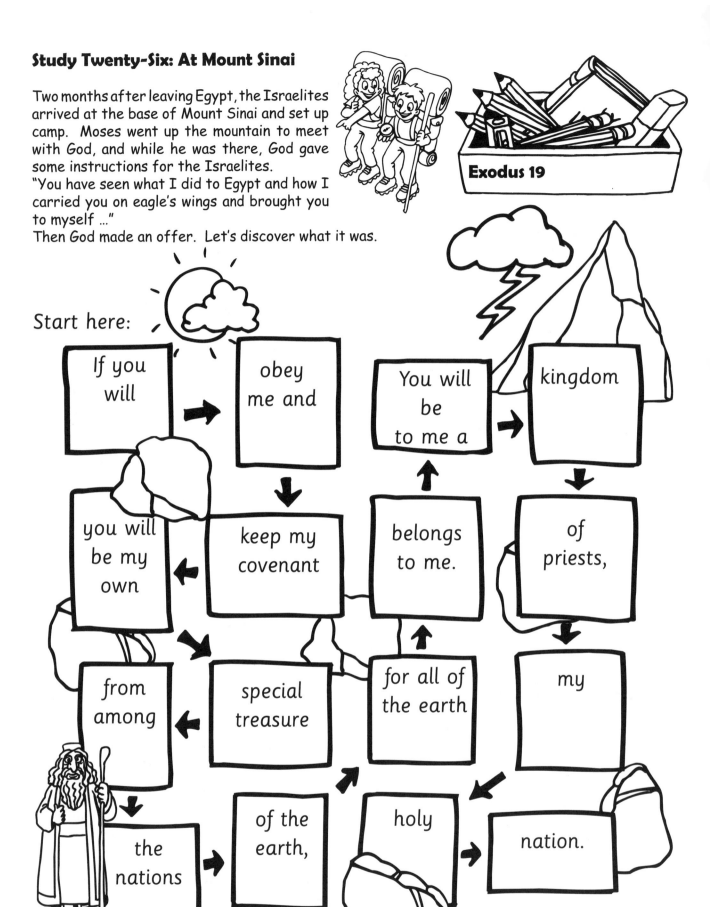

Start here:

| If you will | obey me and | You will be to me a | kingdom |
| you will be my own | keep my covenant | belongs to me. | of priests, |
| from among | special treasure | for all of the earth | my |
| the nations | of the earth, | holy | nation. |

When Moses came back down the mountain and told the people what God had said, they all agreed, "We will do everything God asks us." Then God said to Moses, "I am going to come to you in a thick cloud so that the people will hear me when I speak to you and will always trust you." God told Moses to prepare the people for his visit. They were to purify themselves and wash their clothes. Then he gave a strict warning. What was it?

Do _ _ _ go _ _ the
_ _ _ _ _ _ _ or
_ _ _ _ _ the _ _ _ _ of
it. Whoever touches the
mountain shall
_ _ _ _ _ _ be put
_ _ _ _ _ _.

death

to

mountain

surely

touch

foot

not

up

It was a serious business. If anyone or any animal touched the mountain, they were to be stoned to death or shot with arrows. Only when they heard the ram's horn blast were they to get together at the foot of the mountain.

On the morning of the third day there was thunder and lightning, and a thick cloud came down over the mountain. A loud horn blast echoed around the camp and everyone trembled. It was time for Moses to lead the people to the foot of the mountain.

God came down onto the mountain in a blaze of fire. Smoke billowed up as if it had come from a furnace and the whole mountain trembled violently. It was awesome. As the horn blasted louder and louder, Moses spoke, and God thundered his reply.

God told Moses to climb to the top of the mountain, where he gave him a message for the Israelites. "Tell the people not to come here or they will die. Even the priests must purify themselves or I will destroy them."

## Study Twenty-Seven: The Ten Commandments

Moses returned to give the people the message, and he gave a set of God's laws for the Israelites to live by. You can find them in the Bible in Exodus chapter 20. Below are ten commandments which God gave Moses, but can you put them in the right order. Follow the wiggly lines, then put the correct number above each box.

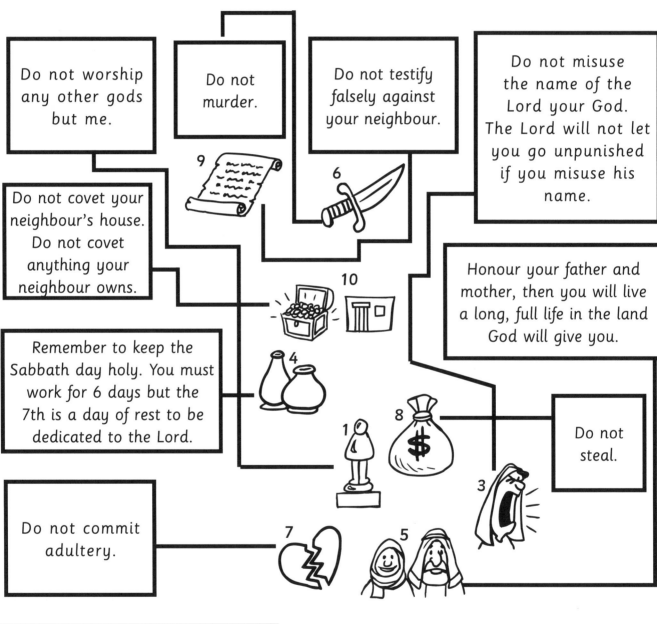

Do not worship any other gods but me.

Do not murder.

Do not testify falsely against your neighbour.

Do not misuse the name of the Lord your God. The Lord will not let you go unpunished if you misuse his name.

Do not covet your neighbour's house. Do not covet anything your neighbour owns.

Remember to keep the Sabbath day holy. You must work for 6 days but the 7th is a day of rest to be dedicated to the Lord.

Honour your father and mother, then you will live a long, full life in the land God will give you.

Do not steal.

Do not commit adultery.

Don't make idols of any kind - whether in the shape of birds animals or fish. You shall not bow down to them or worship them. For I am a jealous God.

When the people heard the thunder and the horn and saw the lightning and smoke, they were very scared. "You tell us what God says and we'll listen," they begged. "But don't let God speak to us directly or we'll die." But Moses reassured them. Click has downloaded a puzzle but the columns have got mixed up. Put the columns in the right order to discover what he said.

| 4 | 13 | 7 | 11 | 5 | 8 | 15 | 6 | 14 | 1 | 12 | 3 | 9 | 2 | 10 |
|---|----|---|----|---|---|----|---|----|---|----|---|---|---|----|
| t | i | e | r |   |   | . | b | d | D | a | n | a | o | f |
|   |   | a | i |   | m |   | c |   | G | n | d | e | o |   |
| s |   | a | o |   | y |   | w |   | t |   | i |   | h | s |
| t | l | o | i |   | u |   | y |   | t | l | a |   | h | w |
| w | a | i | r |   | s |   | h | t | k | e | o |   | n | g |
| e | o | T |   | r | h | r | . | u | p | y | w | e | o | n |
| r |   | f | m |   |   |   | o |   | f |   | a | h | e | i |
| l |   | e | t |   | l |   | h |   | w | o | l | p | i |   |
| p | m | o | r |   | u |   | y |   | k | o | e |   | e | f |
| n |   | g |   | i |   |   | n |   | s |   | n |   | i |   |

| 1 | 2 | 3 | 4 | 5 | 6 | 7 | 8 | 9 | 10 | 11 | 12 | 13 | 14 | 15 |
|---|---|---|---|---|---|---|---|---|----|----|----|----|----|----|
|   |   |   |   |   |   |   |   |   |    |    |    |    |    |    |
|   |   |   |   |   |   |   |   |   |    |    |    |    |    |    |
|   |   |   |   |   |   |   |   |   |    |    |    |    |    |    |
|   |   |   |   |   |   |   |   |   |    |    |    |    |    |    |
|   |   |   |   |   |   |   |   |   |    |    |    |    |    |    |
|   |   |   |   |   |   |   |   |   |    |    |    |    |    |    |
|   |   |   |   |   |   |   |   |   |    |    |    |    |    |    |
|   |   |   |   |   |   |   |   |   |    |    |    |    |    |    |
|   |   |   |   |   |   |   |   |   |    |    |    |    |    |    |
|   |   |   |   |   |   |   |   |   |    |    |    |    |    |    |
|   |   |   |   |   |   |   |   |   |    |    |    |    |    |    |

Moses left the people and went into thick darkness where God was. And while he was there, God gave him laws, which the Israelites were to follow. And when Moses came out and told the people what God had said, they all agreed to follow God's instructions.

47

## Study Twenty-Eight: Moses and the Mountain

Early the next morning, Moses set to work to build an altar at the foot of the mountain. He set up twelve stone pillars, representing the tribes of Israel, and burnt offerings and sacrifices were made to God. Then Moses took the book of the covenant and read it to the people, and they all agreed to obey everything that God had commanded. A while later, God told Moses to come up the mountain again. He was going to give Moses some tablets of stone on which he had written his instructions and commands. So Moses climbed the mountain, taking an assistant with him. Click has printed out a puzzle for us because we need to work out the name of the assistant. Look at the circle below, and take the first letter of each object. Then work out which letter should be the first letter of this person's name and carry on round the circle in a clockwise direction. Write the name in the space provided.

Exodus 24: 4-17

HOLY BIBLE

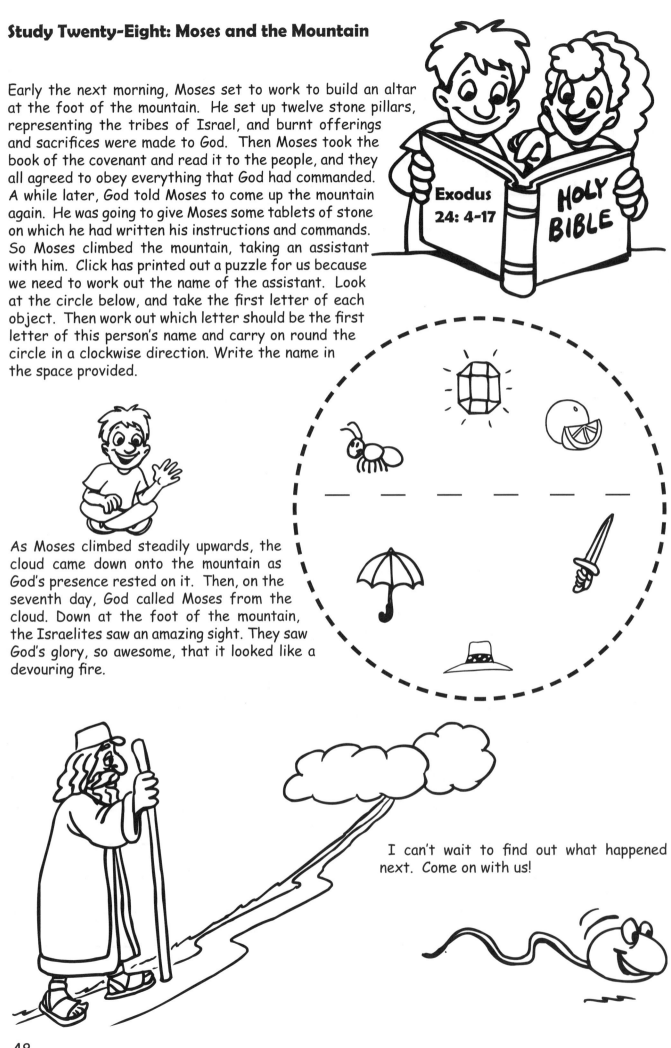

As Moses climbed steadily upwards, the cloud came down onto the mountain as God's presence rested on it. Then, on the seventh day, God called Moses from the cloud. Down at the foot of the mountain, the Israelites saw an amazing sight. They saw God's glory, so awesome, that it looked like a devouring fire.

I can't wait to find out what happened next. Come on with us!

## Study Twenty-Nine: The Ark

We've been finding out what happened while Moses was meeting with God at Mount Sinai. God wanted the Israelites to build a special place (a sanctuary) where he could live among them. It was to be called a tabernacle, and there were very clear instructions about what was to go inside it. But first, the Israelites were to bring offerings to God, which would be used to build it.

**Exodus 25**

Gold, silver, bronze, blue, purple and scarlet yarn, linen, goat hair, ram skins (dyed red), hides (of sea cows), acacia wood, olive oil, spices, onyx stones.

> Can you find these words in the wordsearch?
> Gold, Silver, Bronze, Yarn, Linen, Goat hair, Ram skins, Hides, Acacia wood, Olive oil, Onyx stones

| E | O | J | A | T | S | E | D | I | H | O | P |
|---|---|---|---|---|---|---|---|---|---|---|---|
| A | N | E | N | I | L | U | S | O | N | A | K |
| C | R | E | Z | N | O | R | B | L | S | E | G |
| A | D | A | C | L | N | I | P | I | X | R | O |
| C | E | J | M | N | R | A | Y | V | O | V | A |
| I | G | S | Y | S | T | U | I | E | R | C | T |
| A | F | E | O | W | K | D | Z | O | E | T | H |
| W | U | C | G | B | N | I | K | I | V | I | A |
| O | W | I | A | O | D | P | N | L | L | S | I |
| O | Z | P | O | N | L | H | O | S | I | X | R |
| D | A | S | M | R | E | D | C | X | S | E | O |
| S | E | N | O | T | S | X | Y | N | O | L | J |

So now let's move on and find out what was to go inside the tabernacle.

49

An  A chest made of acacia wood and overlaid with gold. Its cover was the place of atonement. This was where the stone tablets would be kept, and it was to be placed behind an inner curtain which would separate the holy place from the most holy place. (Atonement means - to make amends for wrong doing or to be forgiven by God for wrong doing.)

A  also made of acacia wood and overlaid with gold. The Israelites were also to make gold plates and dishes, pitchers and bowls to be used for drink offerings. The Bread of Presence was to be kept on the table before God at all times.

A  to be made of gold and with three branches on either side of the centre stem. Also needed were gold snuffers and olive oil to burn day and night.

An

This was made of acacia wood and had a horn at each of the four corners. It was to be overlaid with bronze. The Israelites were also to make ash buckets, shovels, basins, meat hooks and fire pans from bronze. Then there was the tabernacle itself. It was to be made from ten sheets of linen, and decorated with blue, purple and scarlet yarn. This was to be attached to a wooden frame and held down with bronze tent pegs. A courtyard for the tabernacle was to be made with curtains held up by bronze posts. And still there was more.

An   was to be built for the burning of incense.

It was to be made of acacia wood, with horns at the corners and to be overlaid with gold.

In addition to this there was to be a

 for Aaron and his sons to wash their hands and feet in before going into the tabernacle to burn offerings.

was to be made of a blend of spices and olive oil. This was a holy oil for anointing the Tabernacle, the Ark of the Covenant, the table and its utensils, the lampstand and its accessories, the incense altar, the altar of burnt offering and its utensils and the washbasin and pedestal. This was not to be poured onto any person. Incense was to be made of sweet spices. It was most holy and was to be reserved for the Lord only.

50

## Study Thirty: The Priestly Garments

God now told Moses to set apart five people to be priests. Can you help us to find out their names?

12am, 12am, 5pm, 2pm, 1pm    and his sons

1pm,12am,3am,12am,1am    and

12am,1am,8am,7am,8pm,    4am,11am,4am,12am,11pm,12am,5pm    and

8am,7pm,7am,12am,12pm,12am,5pm

Everyone with special skills as tailors were instructed to make holy garments (tunics, turbans etc) which would set Aaron apart from the rest. His sons would have special clothes too. Click has printed out a picture of Aaron's clothing. Let's take a look and crack the code to work out what was to be worn.

a=1, b=2, c=3, d=4, e=5, f=6, g=7,h=8,i=9,j=10, k=11, l=12, m=13, n=14, o=15, p=16, q=17, r=18, s=19, t=20, u=21, v=22, w=23, x=24, y=25, z =26

1) 2, 18,5, 1,19,20,16,9,5,3,5    2) 5,16,8,15,4

3) 18,15,2,5                          4) 23,15,22,5,14  20,21,14,9,3

5) 20,21,18,2,1,14                    6) 19,1,19,8

The craftsmen had to take two onyx stones and engrave on them the names of the sons of Israel in the order of their birth – six names on each stone. These were to be mounted in gold filigree settings and fastened onto the shoulder pieces of the ephod as memorial stones. On the breastpiece there were to be four rows of three different precious stones. Each stone would represent one of the sons of Israel. Turn over the page and see if you can you work out where they went?

R_by
21

Top_z
1

B_ryl
5

Tu_qu_ise
18  15

Sa_ph_re
16  9

Eme_ _ld
18  1

Ja_i_th
3  14

Agat_
5

Am_thyst
5

C_rysol_te
8  9

O_yx
14

Ja_per
19

To give you a helping hand Click has also put in some number clues to help you complete the words. There were lots more instructions, and we've discovered that there was a reason behind everything that was to be made, for example, gold bells were to be put around the hem of the robe so that when Aaron came into the Holy Place before God, their tinkling would announce that he was coming. Why don't you turn to Exodus chapter 28 and find out even more.

## Study Thirty-One: The Calf of Gold

Moses spent forty days and nights on the mountain. God gave him clear instructions for making the tabernacle and clothing for the priests. He also told him about how to set apart and make priests, and what their duties should be. But bad things were happening in the Israelite camp. You see, with each passing day, the people got more restless, and instead of trusting God and waiting patiently for Moses they went to Aaron and complained.

It's been a long time since Moses went up the mountain. We don't know what's happened to him. Make us some gods to lead us.

Aaron gave way and blew it big time.

Tell your families to take off their gold earrings and bring them to me.

Everyone obeyed Aaron, who took the gold, melted it down, and made it into the shape of an animal. What animal was it? Match the shape to find out.

This was the sort of idol that was worshipped back in Egypt. Aaron built an altar in front of the calf and announced

Tomorrow we will have a festival.

The next day, the people got up early and began to offer sacrifices to the calf. Had they forgotten what God had done for them? Did they think that God couldn't see them? Of course he could. God was so angry that he decided to destroy the people and make Moses into a great nation instead. Full of dismay, Moses pleaded with God not to do it. He reminded him of the promise made to Abraham, Isaac and Jacob. What was it?

👁 will make 〰➡ ✋ as ⏱

as the ☆ in the ☁

and 👁 will give them all

this 🌲 that 👁 / them.

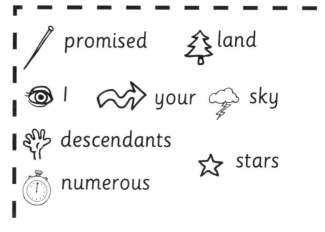

/ promised    🌲 land

👁 I   〰➡ your   ☁ sky

✋ descendants

☆ stars

⏱ numerous

Moses said to God...

> If you destroy everyone now, the Egyptians will say that you only brought the Israelites out of Egypt to destroy them.

It must have been a big relief to Moses when God didn't punish the people with the disaster he had threatened.    So what did happen?

Well, Moses went back down the mountain, carrying the two stone tablets with God's writing engraved on them.  Joshua, who was with him, heard the noise of the people below, but didn't know what was happening. "There is the sound of war in the camp," he said to Moses.  What did Moses reply?  Count two letters back to find out.

It's not a cry of  x,k,e,v,q,t,a.

It's not a cry of f,g,h,g,c,v.

It's the sound of a  e,g,n,g,d,t,  c,v,k,q,p.

The two men came near to the camp, and when Moses saw all that was going on, he was furious.  Throwing the stone tablets to the ground and smashing them, he stormed forward.   The golden calf was melted down, and when it had cooled it was ground to powder and mixed with water.  Then the people had to drink it. Moses turned to Aaron and demanded...

> What did these people do to you to make you lead them into such sin?

But Aaron could only make weak excuses. "When the people asked me to make gods to help them, I told them to bring their gold earrings.  I threw the earrings into the fire and out came this calf!"

It was a disaster.  The people were out of control and their behaviour had caused great amusement to their enemies.  Moses took immediate action. "All of you who are on the Lord's side, come here and join me," he demanded.  All the Levites came.  Then Moses said, "This is what God says.  Strap on your swords and go through the camp killing your brothers, friends and neighbours."  The Levites obeyed, and that day, around three thousand people died.  Then Moses said to the Levites, "Today you have been set aside for the service of the Lord, because you obeyed him even though it meant killing members of your family. God is going to bless you greatly. God also sent a great plague on the Israelites because of what they had done.  It was a terrible lesson to learn.

## Study Thirty-Two: The People are Sorry

God spoke again, his words must have really worried Moses. Start at the centre with the letter G and move anti-clockwise to find out what God said.

**Exodus 33**

_____

_____

| | | | | | | | | | | |
|---|---|---|---|---|---|---|---|---|---|---|
| S | E | D | T | H | G | I | M | I | D | N |
| T | Y | E | S | U | A | C | E | B | U | A |
| R | O | . | Y | E | N | O | H | D | O | E |
| O | U | B | W | O | L | F | D | N | Y | L |
| Y | A | U | I | T | P | U | N | A | H | P |
| Y | R | T | N | O | G | O | A | K | T | O |
| O | E | I | G | T | H | E | L | L | I | E |
| U | A | W | W | I | T | H | M | I | W | P |
| O | S | I | L | L | N | O | T | G | O | D |
| N | T | I | F | F | - | N | E | C | K | E |
| T | H | E | W | A | Y | . | * | * | * | * |

When the people heard this they began to mourn and no-one put on any jewellery. Moses went outside the camp and into a tent where he would often meet with God. He said to God,

How will anyone know that you are pleased with me and with your people unless you go with us? What else will show that I and your people are different from everyone else?

Then God relented. He said, "I will do as you have asked because I am pleased with you and I know you by name."

Moses made a request, then. "Please show me your glory," he asked, and God replied,

THERE IS A PLACE WHERE YOU MAY STA**N**D **O**N A R**O**CK. I WILL PUT YOU **IN** TH**E** CLEFT OF THE ROCK AND COVER YOU WITH **M**Y H**A**ND UNTIL M**Y** GLORY HA**S** PASS**E**D BY. TH**E**N I WILL RE**M**O**V**E MY H**A**ND A**N**D YOU WILL SEE ME FROM BEHIND. BUT YOU WILL NOT SEE MY FAC**E**.

Take each highlighted letter and put it into order to find out why.

_ _   _ _ _   _ _ _   _ _ _   _ _   _ _ _   _ _ ᵛ _.

## Study Thirty-Three: A New Copy of the Covenant

Once again Moses found himself being called by God to go up Mount Sinai. But first, he had to prepare two stone tablets like the first ones.

Exodus 34

God said, "Be ready to come up in the morning. No-one else may come with you. No-one, man or beast is allowed anywhere on the mountain."

Moses set off up the mountain carrying the tablets in his hands. God came down in a pillar of cloud. He passed in front of the mountain and said,

I am the Lord, the merciful and gracious God. I am slow to anger and rich in unfailing love to many thousands by forgiving every kind of sin and rebellion. Even so, I do not leave sin unpunished.

Moses fell to the ground and worshipped. He said, "Please go with us. I know we are unruly and stubborn, but please forgive us and accept us as your own special possession." So God made a covenant:

I will    that have    done before    the earth    any nation.    around you    the power    I will    through

never been    perform wonders    or in    anywhere in all    will see    All the people    display    of the Lord    you.

I will _ _ _ _ _ _ _ _ _ _ _ _ _ _ _ _ that have _ _ _ _ _ _ _ _ _ done before

_ _ _ _ _ _ _ _ _ _ _ _ _ _ _ the earth _ _ _ _ any nation. _ _ _ _ _ _

_ _ _ _ _ _ around you _ _ _ _ _ _ _ the power _ _ _ _ _ _ _ _ _ I will display

_ _ _ _ _ _ _ _ _ _ .

God promised the Israelites that if they obeyed the commands he gave them, he would drive out everyone who stood in their way. Moses was on the mountain with God for forty days and forty nights, and during that time he didn't eat or drink. While he was there, he wrote the Ten Commandments on the stone tablets. When he came back down his face was radiant because he had spoken with the Lord. Moses gave them the instructions that God had given to him. Moses had to cover his face with a veil.

## Study Thirty-Four: Further Instructions

Moses called the people together and said, "You must only work for six days each week. The seventh is a holy day that belongs to the Lord. Anyone who works on that day will die. Then he invited the people to bring offerings to the Lord, and they went away to their tents to prepare their gifts. Everyone who wanted to help, whether sewing or

spinning, or giving acacia wood, jewellery or other things brought their offerings to God.

Then Moses told the people that God had chosen a man and had given him skill in all kinds of crafts. He had been filled with the spirit of God, who had given him great wisdom and intelligence. Let's find out his name.

_ _ _ _ _ _ _ _ son of _ _ _ grandson of _ _ _ of the tribe of _ _ _ _ _.

God had given to him, and another man, the ability to teach their skills to others. Let's find out who the other man was.

_ _ _ _ _ _ _ son of _ _ _ _ _ _ _ _ _ _ _ of the tribe of _ _ _.

These men and other craftsmen gifted by God as jewellers, designers, weavers, embroiderers and other skills were instructed to construct and furnish the Tabernacle as God had commanded. When the Tabernacle and all the priestly clothing had been finished, everything was brought to Moses. From the Ark of the Covenant and the table and its utensils, to the altars, the curtains and the priestly clothing, everything was inspected. Everything had been done just as God had commanded and so Moses blessed them.

## Study Thirty-Five: The Tabernacle Completed

And so, Detectives, we have almost come to the end of Exodus. On the first day of the first month the Tabernacle was set up, and everything that God had commanded was placed inside. When everything had been set up, the cloud came down and covered the Tent of Meeting, and the glory of the Lord filled the Tabernacle.

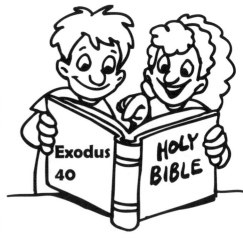

Whenever the cloud lifted from the tabernacle, the Israelites would move on, but if the cloud didn't lift, they stayed. The cloud of the Lord covered the tabernacle by day, and fire was in the cloud at night. Click has printed out a crossword to see how much we can remember.

## CROSSWORD

## Across

2. The means by which the names of the sons of Israel were put on to the onyx stones.
7. One of the gemstones on the priest's breastpiece.
9. It was to be on the table before God at all times.
10. The contents of the bronze basin used by the priests.
13. The place where the stone tablets were to be stored.
16. Made with acacia wood and overlaid with gold.
18. An article of clothing worn by the priest.
21. Used for drinking from.
22. The place for burning incense.
24. Two onyx ones.
25. Embroidered clothing worn by the priests.
26. Animals used for burnt offerings.
27. It was bronze and filled with water.
29. Made of acacia wood with four horns in each corner and overlaid with bronze.
30. The ark's cover was this.

## Down

1. The sanctuary where God would live among the Israelites.
2. One of the gemstones on the priest's breastpiece.
3. Moses met with him on Mount Sinai.
4. Moses' face covering.
5. The Ark was one.
6. The first ones smashed.
8. One of the gemstones on the priest's breastpiece.
11. A type of offering NOT to be made on the altar of incense.
12. Used to separate the holy place from the most holy place.
14. Made of gold and used for burning olive oil.
15. The washbasin was placed on it.
17. The priests were to wear them.
19. Made by blending olive oil and spices.
20. To go on the table.
23. An area for the tabernacle enclosed by curtains.
28. The type of linen used for the ephod.

JESUS FACT FILE:

The story of Moses and the Israelites doesn't end here of course. Moses is mentioned many times in the New Testament as well as in the Old. When Jesus and three of his disciples went up a mountain one day a great miracle took place. Jesus himself spoke with Moses and Elijah on the mountain even though both men had been in heaven for many years. And then when an even more amazing miracle happened and Jesus rose from the dead he spent some time teaching two disciples by showing them how Christ's death had all been part of God's amazing plan. How did he teach them? He used the Old Testament and the words of Moses.

## Study Thirty-Six: Graduation Quiz

Now just in case you thought that the book was finished Click the Mouse has decided to print out for you a special Bible Detectives Quiz on Exodus

Who did the Israelites ask for gold and silver?
What meal did Jesus celebrate with his disciples before his death?
Who said he would fight for the Israelites?
What did the pillar of cloud change into at night?
What did Moses throw on top of the bitter water?
What birds did God send to the Israelite camp?
What did Moses use to get water out of the rock?

Who held up Moses' arms during the Amalekite battle?
Who were Moses' sons?
What mountain did Moses climb to meet with God?
How many commands did God give the Israelites?
Who was Moses' assistant?
What colours would you have seen in the special sanctuary?
How many jewels were on the priest's breastplate?

What was the idol that the Israelites worshipped?
When the Israelites repented of their sin what did they not wear?
What happened to Moses' face when he met with God?
How many days in the week were the Israelites allowed to work?
Who did the seventh day belong to?
On what day of the week was the tabernacle set up?
What came down and covered the tent of meeting?

# Certificate of Recognition

As an official member of the
Bible Detectives Squad
you have been awarded this certificate
to mark an excellent result!

Name: _____

Investigation: _____

Commenced on: _____

Completed on: _____

Signature: _____

ANSWERS

**PAGE 3** Reuben, Simeon, Levi, Issachar, Dan, Asher, Naphtali, Judah, Zebulun, Gad, Benjamin. **PAGE 4** Joseph and his brothers died. But their descendants had many children and grandchildren. They multiplied quickly and soon filled the land./ Pithom and Rameses. **PAGE 5** Kill all the boys as soon as they are born./ But because they feared God they disobeyed the king and let the boys live. **PAGE 6** Pharaoh gave an order to all his people to throw all the newborn Israelite boys into the Nile. **PAGE 8** Moses' big sister Miriam./ Take this child home and nurse him for me. I will pay you for your help. **PAGE 10** (1)Zebulun, (2) Israelites, (3) Pithom, (4) Princess, (5) order, (6) reeds, (7) arrested, (8)Hebrew. Vertical column reads "Zipporah"./ Gershom. **PAGE 11** Do not come any closer. Take off your sandals, for you are standing on holy ground. **PAGE 12** I will be with you. And this will be the sign to you that it is I who have sent you. When you have brought the people out of Egypt you will worship God on this mountain./ Canaanites, Hittites, Amorites, Hivites and Jebusites. **PAGE 13** Perizzites/ Let us take a three-day journey into the desert to offer sacrifices to our God. **PAGE 15** I will help you speak and will teach you what to say./ God said Aaron will speak to the people for you and it will be as if he were your mouth and as if you were God to him. But take your staff with you so that you can perform miraculous signs with it. **PAGE 16** Israel is my firstborn son. I commanded you to let him go so he could worship me. But as you refused to let him go, I will kill your firstborn son. **PAGE 17** Go into the desert to meet Moses./ When they heard that the Lord was concerned about them and had seen their misery they bowed down and worshipped. **PAGE 18** Who is the Lord that I should obey him and let Israel go? I do not know the Lord and I will not let Israel go. **PAGE 19** I will make you my own special people and I will be your God. Then you will know that I am the Lord your God who has rescued you from slavery in Egypt. **PAGE 20** Aaron's snake swallowed up all the others. **PAGE 21** In the morning go to the river Nile with your staff and wait for Pharaoh to come./Word search **PAGE 23** This is the finger of God/ A plague of flies/ Be sure you don't change your mind again. **PAGE 24** I have raised you up for this purpose that I might show you my power and that my name might be made known in all the earth. **PAGE 25** (1) finger (2) ovens (3) flies (4) three (5) river (6) Nile. - Goshen. **PAGE 26** locusts/ A West wind came and blew the locusts into the Red sea. **PAGE 27** Master Detective Quiz: 39, Joseph, Pithom, Rameses, Midwives, Joachabed and Amram, He killed an Egyptian, Midian, Zipporah, Burning bush, Turned it into a snake, straw, Aaron, Frogs, Gnats, Flies, Locusts. **PAGE 28** The Israelites asked their Egyptian neighbours for articles of gold and silver. **PAGE 29** Do not be afraid. Stay where you are because today God will rescue you. The Egyptians you see today you will never see again. The Lrod will fight for you just be still. **PAGE 31** Go away! Leave us all of you. Go and worship the Lord. Take your flocks and herds and give me a blessing./They followed a pillar of fire at night and a pillar of cloud by day. **PAGE 33** Hold your staff out over the water. A path will open up through the sea. **PAGE 35** Miriam, East, Grumbled, Danced, Shur - Marah/ If you listen carefully to the Lord your God and do what is right in his sight, if you obey his commands and laws then I will not make you suffer the diseases I sent on the Egyptians, for I am the Lord who heals you. **PAGE 36** 1 and 7, 2 and 8, 3 and 5, 4 and 6 **PAGE 37** The Lord will give you meat to eat in the evening and bread in the morning. Page 38 It was full of maggots and began to smell. **PAGE 39** Get a jar and put an omer of manna into it. Then store it in a sacred place as a reminder for all future generations **PAGE 40** Massah, Meribah **PAGE 42** Zipporah, Gershom, Eliezer/ Now I know that the Lord is greater than all other gods. **PAGE 43** Home in Peace **PAGE 44** If you will obey me and keep my covenant you will be my own special treasure from among the nations of the earth, for all of the earth belongs to me. You will be to me a kingdom of priests, my holy nation. **PAGE 45** Do not go up the mountain or touch the foot of it. Whoever touches the mountain shall surely be put to death. **PAGE 46** 1. Do not worship any other Gods but me, 2. Do not make idols of any kind 3. Do not misuse the name of the Lord your God 4. Remember to keep the Sabbath day holy. 5. Honour your father and mother. 6. Do not murder. 7. Do not commit adultary. 8. Do not steal. 9. Do not testify falsely against your neighbour. 10. Do not covet. Page 47 Don't be afraid. God came in this way so that you will know his great power. Then your fear of him will help to keep you from sinning. **PAGE 48** Joshua Page 49 Wordsearch **PAGE 50** Ark, Table, Lampstand, Atar of burnt offering, Incense altar, Bronze Washbasin, Anointing oil, Incense. **PAGE 51** Aaron, Nadab, Abihu, Eleazar, Ithamar/ (1) a breastpiece, (2) an ephod (3) a robe (4) a woven tunic (5) a turban (6) a sash. **PAGE 52** 1st row – ruby, topaz, beryl, 2nd row – turquoise, sapphire, emerald 3rd row – jacionth, agate, amethyst, 4th row – chrysolite, onyx, jasper. **PAGE 53** I will make your descendants as numerous as the stars in the sky and I will give them all this land that I promised them **PAGE 54** It's not a cry of victory, It's not a cry of defeat, It's the sound of a celebration. **PAGE 55** Go up to the land flowing with milk and honey. But I will not go with you, because you are a stiff necked people and I might destroy you on th=e way/ No one may see me and live. **PAGE 56** I will perform wonders that have never been done before anywhere in all the earth or in any nation. All the people around you will see the power of the Lord I will display through you. **PAGE 57** Bezalel son of Uri, grandson on Hur, of the tribe of Judah, Oholiab son of Ahisamach of the tribe of Dan. **PAGE 58** Across – (2) engraved (7) jacinth (9) bread (10) water (12) inner curtain (13) Ark of the Covenant (16) table (18) ephod (21) cup (22) Incense Altar (24) stones (26) rams (25) tunics (27) washbasin (29) Altar of Burnt Offering (30) Place of Atonement. Down - (1) tabernacle (2) emerald (3) God (4) veil (5) chest (6) stone tablets (8) agate (11) grain (14) lampstand (15) pedestal (17) holy garments (19) anointing oil (20) utensils (23) courtyard (28) fine **PAGE 60** Their Egyptian neighbours; The passover; God; A pillar of fire; A piece of wood; Quail; His staff; Aaron and Hur; Gershom and Eliezer; Mount Sinai; Ten; Joshua; Gold, Silver, Bronze, Blue, Purple, Scarlet; Twelve; Golden calf; Jewelery; It shone; Six; God; First day of the month; A cloud.

wordsearch page 49

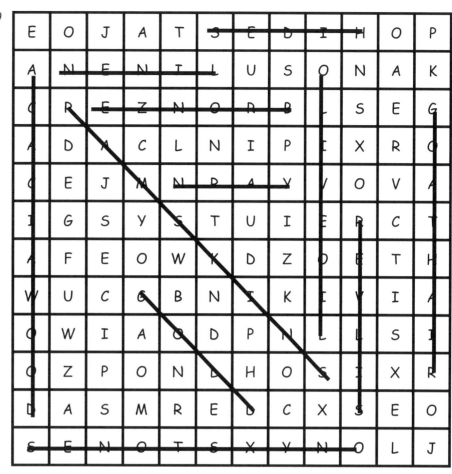

| E | O | J | A | T | S | E | D | I | H | O | P |
|---|---|---|---|---|---|---|---|---|---|---|---|
| A | N | E | N | I | L | U | S | O | N | A | K |
| G | R | E | Z | N | O | R | B | L | S | E | G |
| A | D | A | C | L | N | I | P | E | X | R | O |
| O | E | J | M | N | R | A | V | V | O | V | A |
| I | G | S | Y | S | T | U | I | E | R | C | T |
| A | F | E | O | W | K | D | Z | O | E | T | H |
| W | U | C | G | B | N | I | K | E | Y | I | A |
| O | W | I | A | O | D | P | N | L | L | S | I |
| O | Z | P | O | N | D | H | O | S | I | X | R |
| D | A | S | M | R | E | D | C | X | S | E | O |
| S | E | N | O | T | S | X | V | N | O | L | J |

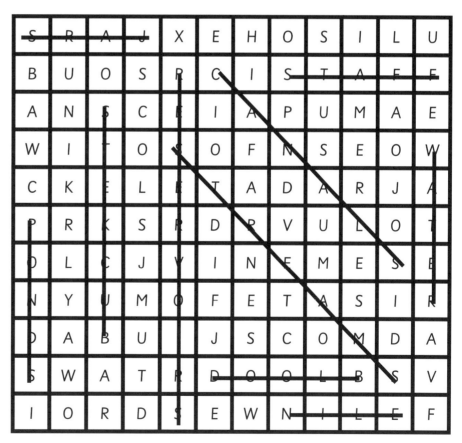

wordsearch page 21

| S | R | A | J | X | E | H | O | S | I | L | U |
|---|---|---|---|---|---|---|---|---|---|---|---|
| B | U | O | S | R | G | I | S | T | A | F | F |
| A | N | S | C | E | I | A | P | U | M | A | E |
| W | I | T | O | S | O | F | N | S | E | O | W |
| C | K | E | L | E | T | A | D | A | R | J | A |
| P | R | K | S | R | D | P | V | U | L | O | T |
| O | L | C | J | V | I | N | E | M | E | S | E |
| N | Y | U | M | O | F | E | T | A | S | I | R |
| D | A | B | U |   | J | S | C | O | M | D | A |
| S | W | A | T | R | D | O | O | L | B | S | V |
| I | O | R | D | S | E | W | N | I | L | E | F |

63

Christian Focus Publications publishes books for adults and children under its three main imprints: Christian Focus, Mentor and Christian Heritage. Our books reflect that God's word is reliable and Jesus is the way to know him, and live for ever with him. Our children's publication list includes a Sunday school curriculum that covers pre-school to early teens; puzzle and activity books. We also publish personal and family devotional titles, biographies and inspirational stories that children will love. If you are looking for quality Bible teaching for children then we have an excellent range of Bible story and age specific theological books. From pre-school to teenage fiction, we have it covered!
Find us at our web page: www.christianfocus.com

Look out for other Bible Detective titles:
Matthew 185792 673 0
Mark 185792 674 9
Luke 185792  758 3
John 185792 759 1
Genesis 1-84550-066-0